Only the

How to Exploit the

Paranoid

Crisis Points That Challenge

Survive

Every Company

Other books by Andrew S. Grove

High Output Management

One-on-One with Andy Grove

Physics and Technology of Semiconductor Devices

But in capitalist reality, as distinguished from its textbook picture, it is not (price) competition which counts but the competition from the new commodity, the new technology, the source of supply, the new type of organization . . . competition which . . . strikes not at the margins . . . of the existing firms but at their foundations and their very lives.

—Joseph A. Schumpeter,
Capitalism, Socialism and Democracy, 1942

Andrew S. Grove

Only the
How to Exploit the
Paranoid
Crisis Points That Challenge
Survive
Every Company

CURRENCY

DOUBLEDAY

New York London Toronto Sydney Auckland

A CURRENCY BOOK
PUBLISHED BY DOUBLEDAY
a division of Random House, Inc.

1540 Broadway, New York, New York 10036
CURRENCY and DOUBLEDAY are trademarks of Doubleday, a division of
Random House, Inc.

Only the Paranoid Survive was originally published in hardcover by Currency, a
division of Bantam Doubleday Dell Publishing Group, Inc., in 1996.

Third-party trademarks and brands are the property of their respective owners.

Book design by Chris Welch

The Library of Congress has cataloged the hardcover edition of this book as follows:
Grove, Andrew S.
Only the paranoid survive: how to exploit the crisis points that challenge every
company / Andrew S. Grove. — 1st ed.
p.   cm.
1. Organizational change.   2. Strategic planning.
3. Technological innovations—Economic aspects.   I. Title.
HD58.8.G765   1996
658.4′06—dc20   96-13509
CIP

ISBN 0-385-48382-1

First Currency Paperback Edition: April 1999

1 3 5 7 9 10 8 6 4 2

Contents

Chapter 4: They're Everywhere

"Strategic inflection points are not a phenomenon of the high-tech industry, nor are they something that only happens to the other guy."

Chapter 5: "Why Not Do It Ourselves?"

"The memory business crisis—and how we dealt with it—is how I learned the meaning of a strategic inflection point."

Chapter 9: The Internet: Signal or Noise? Threat or Promise?   165

"Anything that can affect industries whose total revenue base is many hundreds of billions of dollars is a big deal."

Chapter 10: Career Inflection Points   185

"Career inflection points caused by a change in the environment do not distinguish between the qualities of the people that they dislodge by their force."

Acknowledgments

The ideas of this book have their origin in two sets of experiences. First and foremost, they are based on my years in management roles at Intel, during which I have experienced a number of strategic inflection points. Second, for the last five years, I have cotaught a course in strategic management at the Stanford University Graduate School of Business where, through the eyes of my students, I got to relive some of my experiences, as well as the experiences of others. The first represents a kind of *in vivo* lesson about managing change; the second, its *in vitro* counterpart.

Correspondingly, my thanks go to those who worked alongside me: my fellow managers at Intel and my students at Stanford. Special thanks go to my coteacher, Professor Robert Burgelman, who, in addition to being my mentor in the art of case teaching, helped me clarify and amplify many of my thoughts.

I had no intention of writing a book on this subject until Harriet Rubin, from Doubleday, sought me out and convinced me that I should do so. Her understanding of the subject, her insistence on clarity and her elaboration of the basic ideas have been very helpful in the development of the manuscript.

Thanks are due to Robert Siegel for his unceasing efforts in locating source reference material for many of my examples, reference material for the notes in the back of this book, and for his nitpicky eyes that ferreted out numerous errors and inconsistencies.

The most significant credit goes to Catherine Fredman, who helped me throughout the long process of transforming a precis into a book. Her understanding of my subject matter, her ability to follow my thought processes, and her incredible organizational skills were immensely valuable. Particularly helpful were her insights into the parallels between individuals' careers and corporate strategy. And her sense of humor has helped me skirt many a pothole.

Last—and definitely not least—my gratitude goes to my wife, Eva, who did double duty. She supported me through decades of navigating changes, many of them quite profound and correspondingly capable of taking their toll. Then she supported me again as I relived some of these events in the pages of this book—and she even helped make sure that my text is clear.

Santa Clara
February 1996

Only the Paranoid Survive

''Sooner or later, something fundamental in your business world will change.''

I'm often credited with the motto, "Only the paranoid survive." I have no idea when I first said this, but the fact remains that, when it comes to business, I believe in the value of paranoia. Business success contains the seeds of its own destruction. The more successful you are, the more people want a chunk of your business and then another chunk and then another until there is nothing left. I believe that the prime responsibility of a manager is to guard constantly against other people's attacks and to inculcate this guardian attitude in the people under his or her management.

The things I tend to be paranoid about vary. I worry about products getting screwed up, and I worry about products getting introduced prematurely. I worry about factories not performing well, and I worry about having too many factories. I worry about hiring the right people, and I worry about morale slacking off.

And, of course, I worry about competitors. I worry about other people figuring out how to do what we do better or cheaper, and displacing us with our customers.

But these worries pale in comparison to how I feel about what I call strategic inflection points.

I'll describe what a strategic inflection point is a bit later in this book. For now, let me just say that a strategic inflection point is a time in the life of a business when its fundamentals are about to change. That change can mean an opportunity to rise to new heights. But it may just as likely signal the beginning of the end.

Strategic inflection points can be caused by technological change but they are more than technological change. They can be caused by competitors but they are more than just competition. They are full-scale changes in the way business is conducted, so that simply adopting new technology or fighting the competition as you used to may be insufficient. They build up force so insidiously that you may have a hard time even putting a finger on what has changed, yet you know that something *has*.

Let's not mince words: A strategic inflection point can be deadly when unattended to. Companies that begin a decline as a result of its changes rarely recover their previous greatness.

But strategic inflection points do not always lead to disaster. When the way business is being conducted changes, it creates opportunities for players who are adept at operating in the new way. This can apply to newcomers or to incumbents, for whom a strategic inflection point may mean an opportunity for a new period of growth.

You can be the subject of a strategic inflection point but you can also be the cause of one. Intel, where I work, has been both. In the mid-eighties, the Japanese memory producers brought upon us an inflection point so overwhelming that it forced us out of memory chips and into the relatively new field of microprocessors. The microprocessor business that we have dedicated ourselves to has since gone on to cause the mother of all inflection points for other companies, bringing very difficult times to the classical mainframe computer industry. Having both been affected by strategic inflection points and having caused them, I can safely say that the former is tougher.

I've grown up in a technological industry. Most of my experiences are rooted there. I think in terms of technological concepts and metaphors, and a lot of my examples in this book come from what I know. But strategic inflection points, while often brought about by the workings of technology, are not restricted to technological industries.

The fact that an automated teller machine could be built has changed banking. If interconnected inexpensive computers can be used in medical diagnosis and consulting, it may change medical care. The possibility that all entertainment content can be created, stored, transmitted and displayed in digital form may change the entire media industry. In short, strategic inflection points are about fundamental change in any business, technological or not.

We live in an age in which the pace of technological change is pulsating ever faster, causing waves that spread outward toward all industries. This increased rate of change will have an impact on you, no matter what you do for a living. It will bring new competition from new ways of doing things, from corners that you don't expect.

It doesn't matter where you live. Long distances used to be a moat that both insulated and isolated people from workers on the other side of the world. But every day, technology narrows that moat inch by inch. Every person in the world is on the verge of becoming both a coworker and a competitor to every one of us, much the same as our colleagues down the hall of the same office building are. Technological change is going to reach out and sooner or later change something fundamental in your business world.

Are such developments a constructive or a destructive force? In my view, they are both. And they are inevitable. In technology, whatever *can* be done *will* be done. We can't stop these changes. We can't hide from them. Instead, we must focus on getting ready for them.

The lessons of dealing with strategic inflection points are similar whether you're dealing with a company or your own career.

If you run a business, you must recognize that no amount of formal planning can anticipate such changes. Does that mean you shouldn't plan? Not at all. You need to plan the way a fire department plans: It cannot anticipate where the next fire will be, so it has to shape an energetic and efficient team that is capable of responding to the unanticipated as well as to any ordinary event. Understanding the nature of strategic inflection points and what to do about them will help you safeguard your company's well-being. It is your responsibility to guide your company out of harm's way and to place it in a position where it can prosper in the new order. Nobody else can do this but you.

If you are an employee, sooner or later you will be affected by a strategic inflection point. Who knows what your job will look like after cataclysmic change sweeps through your industry and engulfs the company you work for? Who knows if your job will even exist and, frankly, who will care besides you?

Until very recently, if you went to work at an established company, you could assume that your job would last the rest of your working life. But when companies no longer have lifelong careers themselves, how can they provide one for their employees?

As these companies struggle to adapt, the methods of doing business that worked very well for them for decades are becoming history. Companies that have had generations of employees growing up under a no-layoff policy are now dumping 10,000 people onto the street at a crack.

The sad news is, nobody owes you a career. Your career is literally your business. You own it as a sole proprietor. You have one employee: yourself. You are in competition with millions of similar businesses: millions of other employees all over the world. You need to accept ownership of your career, your skills and the timing of your moves. It is your responsibility to protect this personal business of yours from harm and to position it to benefit from the changes in the environment. Nobody else can do that for you.

Having been a manager at Intel for many years, I've made myself a student of strategic inflection points. Thinking about them has helped our business survive in an increasingly competitive environment. I'm an engineer and a manager, but I have always had an urge to teach, to share with others what I've figured out for myself. It is that same urge that makes me want to share the lessons I've learned.

This book is not a memoir. I am involved in managing a business and deal daily with customers and partners, and speculate constantly about the intentions of competitors. In writing this book, I sometimes draw on observations I have made through such interactions. But these encounters didn't take place with the notion that they would make it into any public arena. They were business discussions that served a purpose for both Intel and others' businesses, and I have to respect that. So please forgive me if some of these stories are camouflaged in generic descriptions and anonymity. It can't be helped.

What this book *is* about is the impact of changing rules. It's about finding your way through uncharted territories. Through examples and reflections on my and others' experiences, I hope to raise your awareness of what it's like to go through cataclysmic changes and to provide a framework in which to deal with them.

As I said, this book is also about careers. As businesses are created on new foundations or are restructured to operate in a new environment, careers are broken or accelerated. I hope this book will give you some ideas of how you can shepherd your own career through these difficult times.

Let's start by parachuting into the middle of a strategic inflection point, when something is changing in a big way, when something is different, yet when you're so busy trying to survive that the significance of the change only becomes clear in retrospect. Painful as it is, let me relive the story of a problem that Intel had with our flagship device, the Pentium processor, in the fall of 1994.

Something Changed

''New rules prevailed now—and they were powerful enough to cost us nearly half a billion dollars.''

I teach a class in strategic management at Stanford University's business school as a part-time departure from my job as president and CEO of Intel Corporation. The way my coteacher, Professor Robert Burgelman, and I normally grade the students is to go through the class roster right after each session and assess each student's class performance while it is still fresh in our memories.

The process was taking a little longer than usual on the morning of November 22, 1994, the Tuesday before Thanksgiving, and I was about to excuse myself to call my office when the phone rang. It was my office calling me. Our head of communications wanted to talk to me—urgently. She wanted to let me know that a CNN crew was coming to Intel. They had heard of the floating point flaw in the Pentium processor and the story was about to blow up.

I have to backtrack here. First, a word about Intel. Intel in 1994 was a $10 billion-plus producer of computer chips, the largest in the world. We were twenty-six years old and in that period of time we had pioneered two of the most important building blocks of modern technology, memory chips and microprocessors. In 1994, most of our business revolved around microprocessors and it revolved very well indeed. We were very profitable, growing at around 30 percent per year.

Nineteen ninety-four was a very special year for us in another way. It was the year in which we were ramping our latest-generation microprocessor, the Pentium processor, into full-scale production. This was a very major undertaking involving hundreds of our direct customers, i.e., computer manufacturers, some of whom enthusiastically endorsed the new technology and some of whom didn't. We were fully committed to it, so we were heavily advertising the product to get the attention of computer buyers. Internally, we geared up manufacturing plants at four different sites around the world. This project was called "Job 1" so all our employees knew where our priorities lay.

In the context of all this, a troubling event happened. Several weeks earlier, some of our employees had found a string of comments on the Internet forum where people interested in Intel products congregate. The comments were under headings like, "Bug in the Pentium FPU." (FPU stands for floating point unit, the part of the chip that does the heavy-duty math.) They were triggered by the observation of a math professor that something wasn't quite right with the mathematical capabilities of the Pentium chip. This professor reported that he had encountered a division error while studying some complex math problems.

We were already familiar with this problem, having encountered it several months earlier. It was due to a minor design error on the chip, which caused a rounding error in division once every nine billion times. At first, we were very concerned about this, so we mounted a major study to try to understand what once every nine billion divisions would mean. We found the results reassuring. For instance, they meant that an average spreadsheet user would run into the problem only once every 27,000 years of spreadsheet use. This is a long time, much longer than it would take for other types of problems which are always encountered in semiconductors to trip up a chip. So while we created and tested ways to correct the defect, we went about our business.

Meanwhile, this Internet discussion came to the attention of the trade press and was described thoroughly and accurately in a front-page article in one of the trade weeklies. The next week it was picked up as a smaller item in other trade papers. And that seemed to be it. That is, until that Tuesday morning before Thanksgiving.

That's when CNN showed up wanting to talk to us, and they seemed all fired up. The producer had opened his preliminary discussion with our public relations people in an aggressive and accusatory tone. As I listened to our head of communications on the phone, it didn't sound good. I picked up my papers and headed back to the office. In fact, it wasn't good. CNN produced a very unpleasant piece, which aired the next day.

In the days after that, every major newspaper started reporting on the story with headlines ranging from "Flaw Undermines Accuracy of Pentium Chips" to "The Pentium Proposition: To Buy or Not to Buy." Television reporters camped outside our headquarters. The Internet message traffic skyrocketed. It seemed that everyone in the United States keyed into this, followed shortly by countries around the world.

Users started to call us asking for replacement chips. Our replacement policy was based on our assessment of the problem. People whose use pattern suggested that they might do a lot of divisions got their chips replaced. Other users we tried to reassure by walking them through our studies and our analyses, offering to send them a white paper that we wrote on this subject. After the first week or so, this dual approach seemed to be working reasonably well. The daily call volumes were decreasing, we were gearing up to refine our replacement procedures and, although the press was still pillorying us, all tangible indicators—from computer sales to replacement requests—showed that we were managing to work our way through this problem.

Then came Monday, December 12. I walked into my office at eight o'clock that morning and in the little clip where my assistant leaves phone messages there was a folded computer printout. It was a wire service report. And as often happens with breaking news it consisted only of the title. It said something to this effect: IBM stops shipments of all Pentium-based computers.

All hell broke loose again. IBM's action was significant because, well, they are IBM. Although in recent years IBM has not been the power they once were in the PC business, they did originate the "IBM PC" and by choosing to base it on Intel's technology, they made Intel's microprocessors preeminent. For most of the thirteen years since the PC's inception, IBM has been the most important player in the industry. So their action got a lot of attention.

The phones started ringing furiously from all quarters. The call volume to our hotline skyrocketed. Our other customers wanted to know what was going on. And their tone, which had been quite constructive the week before, became confused and anxious. We were back on the defensive again in a major way.

A lot of the people involved in handling this stuff had only joined Intel in the last ten years or so, during which time our business had grown steadily. Their experience had been that working hard, putting one foot in front of the other, was what it took to get a good outcome. Now, all of a sudden, instead of predictable success, nothing was predictable. Our people, while they were busting their butts, were also perturbed and even scared.

And there was another dimension to this problem. It didn't stop at the doors of Intel. When they went home, our employees had to face their friends and their families, who gave them strange looks, sort of accusing, sort of wondering, sort of like, "What are you all doing? I saw such and such on TV and they said your company is greedy and arrogant." Our employees were used to hearing nothing but positive remarks when they said that they worked at Intel. Now they were hearing deprecating jokes like, "What do you get when you cross a mathematician with a Pentium? A mad scientist." And you couldn't get away from it. At every family dinner, at every holiday party, this was the subject of discussion. This change was hard on them, and it scarcely helped their spirits when they had to go back the next morning to answer telephone hotlines, turn production lines on their heads and the like.

I wasn't having a wonderful time either. I've been around this industry for thirty years and at Intel since its inception, and I have survived some very difficult business situations, but this was different. It was much harsher than the others. In fact, it was unlike any of the others at every step. It was unfamiliar and rough territory. I worked hard during the day but when I headed home I got instantly depressed. I felt we were under siege—under unrelenting bombardment. Why was this happening?!

Conference room 528, which is located twenty feet from my office, became the Intel war room. The oval table there is meant to seat about twelve people, but at several times each day more than thirty people were jammed in the room, sitting on the credenza, standing against the wall, coming and going, bringing missives from the front and leaving to execute agreed-upon courses of action.

After a number of days of struggling against the tide of public opinion, of dealing with the phone calls and the abusive editorials, it became clear that we had to make a major change.

The next Monday, December 19, we changed our policy completely. We decided to replace anybody's part who wanted it replaced, whether they were doing statistical analysis or playing computer games. This was no minor decision. We had shipped millions of these chips by now and none of us could even guess how many of them would come back—maybe just a few, or maybe all of them.

In a matter of days, we built up a major organization practically from scratch to answer the flood of phone calls. We had not been in the consumer business in any big way before, so dealing with consumer questions was not something we had ever had to do.

Now, suddenly, we did from one day to another and on a fairly major scale. Our staffing first came from volunteers, from people who worked in different areas of Intel—designers, marketing people, software engineers. They all dropped what they were doing, sat at makeshift desks, answered phones and took down names and addresses. We began to systematically oversee the business of replacing people's chips by the hundreds of thousands. We developed a logistics system to track these hundreds of thousands of chips coming and going. We created a service network to handle the physical replacement for people who didn't want to do it themselves.

Back in the summer when we had first found the floating point flaw, we had corrected the chip design, checked it out very thoroughly to make sure the change didn't produce any new problems, and had already started to phase the corrected version into manufacturing by the time these events took place. We now accelerated this conversion by canceling the usual Christmas shutdown in our factories, and speeded things up even further by pulling the old material off the line and junking it all.

Ultimately, we took a huge write-off—to the tune of $475 million. The write-off consisted of the estimates of the replacement parts plus the value of the materials we pulled off the line. It was the equivalent of half a year's R&D budget or five years' worth of the Pentium processor's advertising spending.

And we embarked on a whole new way of doing business.

What happened here? Something big, something different, something unexpected.

For twenty-six years, every day that we did business, *we* decided what was good and what wasn't when it came to our own product. *We* set our own quality levels and our own specifications, and shipped when *we* decided a product met our own criteria. After all, *we* had designed and conceived these products, and along with the product came our implicit right—and obligation—to decide when the product was good and when it wasn't. Nobody ever questioned that we had the right to do that and generally we were on target. Over twenty-six years, we pioneered one classic product after another: DRAMs, other types of memory chips, microprocessors, computers on a board. Our products had become the basic building blocks of digital electronics. But now, all of a sudden, we were getting strange looks from everyone that seemed to say, "Where do you get off telling us what's good for us?"

Furthermore, since we generally don't sell microprocessors to computer *users* but to computer *makers,* whatever problems we had in the past, we used to handle with the computer manufacturers, engineer to engineer, in conference rooms with blackboards, based on data analyses. But now, all of a sudden, 25,000 computer *users* were calling us every day, saying, "Give me a new part, period." We found ourselves dealing with people who bought nothing directly from us yet were very angry with us.

What was the hardest to take was the outside world's image of us. I still thought of us as a creative, dynamic start-up that had just grown a bit bigger than the other creative, dynamic start-ups. We could still turn on a dime. Our people still put the interests of the company ahead of their own interests and, when problems arose, employees from all different divisions would still rally around and put in incredible hours without anyone ordering them to do so. Yet now the world seemed to treat us like some typical mammoth corporation. And, in the public view, this corporation was giving people the runaround. That outside image didn't jibe with my view of us.

What had happened? And why now? What was different this time? *Something* was, but in the middle of those events it was hard to tell what.

What Happened to Us

A year or so later, as I reflect on it, I see two big long-term forces doing their work on us, creating the conditions in which a tiny flaw in a microprocessor's floating point unit could mushroom into half a billion dollars' worth of damage in less than six weeks.

The first involved our attempting to change how our products were perceived. A few years back, we had introduced a major marketing campaign, the "Intel Inside" program. It was the biggest campaign the industry had ever seen—in fact, it ranks up there with big-time consumer merchandising campaigns. Its aim was to suggest to the computer user that the microprocessor that's inside his or her computer *is* the computer.

Like all good merchandising campaigns, this had the advantage of reinforcing the truth. Even before the campaign, when you asked someone what kind of a computer he had, the first thing he tended to say was, "I have a 386"—which was the microprocessor chip inside the computer—and then he would go on to identify the computer manufacturer, what kind of software it had and so on. Computer users knew instinctively that the identity and class of the computer were determined more than anything else by the microprocessor within. This was obviously very good for us. It gave us distinction, an identity, and helped build computer-user communities' awareness of us and our products.

We aimed our campaign at driving this point home to a wider consumer base and to future computer buyers. We created a distinctive logo and we worked with manufacturers who used our microprocessor in their product to display this logo in their advertising, often with a sticker on the actual computer. Hundreds of manufacturers, domestic and international, participated in this campaign.

We spent a lot of money ourselves promoting this brand. We had billboards displaying the "Intel Inside" logo all over the world and we ran television commercials in many languages. We had even distributed many thousands of "Intel Inside" bicycle reflectors in China. By 1994 our research showed that our logo had become one of the most recognized logos in consumer merchandising, up there with names like Coca-Cola or Nike. So when problems developed with our flagship Pentium chip, our merchandising pointed the users directly back to us.

The second fundamental factor in creating the conditions for the maelstrom was our sheer size. Over the years, we had become the world's largest semiconductor manufacturer. We surpassed the large United States producers, companies we used to consider mammoth and gigantic compared to us just a few years ago, and we surpassed the major Japanese producers who just ten years ago had threatened to put us out of business (more about that in Chapter 5). And we were still growing fast—faster than most large companies. We had also become bigger than most of our customers, companies that I remembered from our earlier years at Intel to be monumentally large corporations. At some point along the way, like a kid who suddenly looks down at his father, our sizes reversed.

This all happened relatively rapidly, in the past decade. And although the recognition of our size fleetingly touched us here and there, largely through the respect we got from other companies in our business, it was hardly something any of us dwelled on. It crept up on us; it just happened.

And now we were dealing with a different and not nearly as pleasant consequence of our huge size and our strong identity. We had become gigantic in the eyes of computer buyers. Unfortunately, it took a blowup to make us realize this.

Given the gradual nature of these changes, which over time added up to a very large change, the old rules of business no longer worked. New rules prevailed now—and they were powerful enough to force us into actions that cost us nearly half a billion dollars.

The trouble was, not only didn't we realize that the rules had changed—what was worse, we didn't know what rules we now had to abide by.

Before this episode, we supplied our computer manufacturer customers well and we guarded the quality of our products as best we knew how. We marketed our products both to the engineers of these computer companies and to computer users. We were fast and agile, as all good start-ups are, we worked hard and everything had worked well in return. But all of a sudden this no longer seemed to be enough.

What happened to us in the course of this event is something that happens to many businesses. All businesses operate by some set of unstated rules and sometimes these rules change—often in very significant ways. Yet there is no flashing sign that heralds these rule changes. They creep up on you as they crept up on us, without warning.

You know only that something has changed, something big, something significant, even if it's not entirely clear what that something is.

It's like sailing a boat when the wind shifts on you but for some reason, maybe because you are down below, you don't even sense that the wind has changed until the boat suddenly heels over. What worked before doesn't work anymore; you need to steer the boat in a different direction quickly before you are in trouble, yet you have to get a feel of the new direction and the strength of the wind before you can hope to right the boat and set a new course. And the tough part is that it is exactly at times like this that hard and definitive actions are required.

Such phenomena are very common. Businesses are about creating change for other businesses. Competition is about creating change; technology is about creating change. The appearance and disappearance of regulations cause further changes. Sometimes these changes affect only a company, other times they affect an entire industry. So the ability to recognize that the winds have shifted and to take appropriate action before you wreck your boat is crucial to the future of an enterprise.

"That Guy Is Always the Last to Know"

In the three months following the Pentium floating point incident, Microsoft's new operating system, Windows 95, was delayed; Apple delayed the release of their new software, Copland; long-standing bugs in both the Windows calculator and Word for Macintosh were highlighted with substantial publicity in trade newspapers; and difficulties associated with Disney's *Lion King* CD-ROM game and Intuit's tax programs all became subjects of daily newspaper coverage. Something changed, not just for Intel but for others in the high-tech business as well.

I don't think this kind of change is a high-tech phenomenon. Examples from industries of all different kinds stare at me from daily newspapers. All the turbulent actions of investments, takeovers and write-offs in the media and telecommunications companies, as well as in banking and healthcare, seem to point to industries in which "something has changed." Technology has something to do with most of these changes only because technology gives companies in each of these industries the power to alter the order around them.

If you work in one of these industries and you are in middle management, you may very well sense the shifting winds on your face before the company as a whole and sometimes before your senior management does. Middle managers—especially those who deal with the outside world, like people in sales—are often the first to realize that what worked before doesn't quite work anymore; that the rules are changing. They usually don't have an easy time explaining it to senior management, so the senior management in a company is sometimes late to realize that the world is changing on them—and the leader is often the last of all to know.

Here's an example: I recently listened to evaluations of a certain highly touted new software from a company whose other products we already use. Our head of Information Technology told of unanticipated obstacles we were running into by trying to adopt this new software and therefore said that she was inclined to wait until the following generation of software was ready. Our marketing manager had heard of the same situation at other companies as well.

I called up the software company's CEO to tell him what I was hearing and asked, "Are you considering changing your strategy and going directly to the new generation?" He said, "No way." They were going to stay the course, they had heard of no one having any problems with their strategy.

When I reported this to the individuals who brought me the news, our IT manager said, "Well, that guy is always the last to know." He, like most CEOs, is in the center of a fortified palace, and news from the outside has to percolate through layers of people from the periphery where the action is. Our IT manager *is* the periphery. Our marketing manager also experiences the skirmishes there.

I was one of the last to understand the implications of the Pentium crisis. It took a barrage of relentless criticism to make me realize that something had changed—and that we needed to adapt to the new environment. We could change our ways and embrace the fact that we had become a household name and a consumer giant, or we could keep our old ways and not only miss an opportunity to nurture new customer relationships but also suffer damage to our corporate reputation and well-being.

The lesson is, we all need to expose ourselves to the winds of change. We need to expose ourselves to our customers, both the ones who are staying with us as well as those that we may lose by sticking to the past. We need to expose ourselves to lower-level employees, who, when encouraged, will tell us a lot that we need to know. We must invite comments even from people whose job it is to constantly evaluate and critique us, such as journalists and members of the financial community. Turn the tables and ask them some questions: about competitors, trends in the industry and what they think we should be most concerned with. As we throw ourselves into raw action, our senses and instincts will rapidly be honed again.

A "10X" Change

''What such a transition does to a business is profound, and how the business manages this transition determines its future.''

We managers like to talk about change, so much that embracing change has become a cliché of management. But a strategic inflection point is not just any change. It compares to change the way Class VI rapids on a river, the kind of deadly and turbulent rapids that even professional rafters approach gingerly, compare to ordinary waters.

We just saw what it's like to be in the middle of a strategic inflection point. Now I'd like to step back and analyze what might cause one.

The Six Forces Affecting a Business

Most analyses of the competitive well-being of businesses are static ones. They describe the relevant forces at any instant in time and help explain how they add up to favorable or unfavorable business positions. But they are of little help when a major change is taking place in the balance of these forces. For instance, traditional competitive analysis doesn't much help us understand the workings of a business when one of these forces grows, say, tenfold in magnitude.

Still, these analyses have provided a good way of describing the factors affecting businesses. Let me start by quickly paraphrasing classical competitive strategy analysis, largely based on the work of Professor Michael Porter of Harvard University, who identified the various forces that determine how competitive a company is. Generations of business people and business students have been trained to think in terms of these forces, so I'll adopt them as our starting point. Porter describes five forces that determine the competitive well-being of a business. In my paraphrasing, they are:

• The power, vigor and competence of a company's existing competitors: Are there a lot of them? Are they well funded? Do they clearly focus on your business?

• The power, vigor and competence of a company's suppliers: Are there a lot of them, so that the business has plenty of choices, or are there few of them, so that they have the business by the throat? Are they aggressive and greedy or are they conservative and guided by the long view toward their customers?

• The power, vigor and competence of a company's customers: Are there a lot of them or is the business dependent on just one or two major customers? Are the customers very demanding, perhaps because *their* business operates under cutthroat competition, or is their business more "gentlemanly"?

• The power, vigor and competence of a company's *potential* competitors: These players are not in the business today but circumstances could change and they might decide to come in; if so, they may be bigger, more competent, better funded and more aggressive than the existing competitors.

• The possibility that your product or service can be built or delivered in a different way. This is often called "substitution," and I've found that this last factor is the most deadly of all. New techniques, new approaches, new technologies can upset the old order, mandate a new set of rules and create an entirely new climate in which to do business. This is what trucking and air transportation have done to railroads, what container shipping has done to traditional ports, what superstores have done to small shops, what microprocessors continue to do to computing and what digital media might do to entertainment.

Recent modifications of competitive theory call attention to a sixth force: the force of complementors. Complementors are other businesses from whom customers buy complementary products. Each company's product works better or sometimes only works with the other company's product. Cars need gasoline; gasoline needs cars. Computers need software; software needs computers.

Complementors often have the same interests as your business and travel the same road. I think of them as "fellow travelers." While your interests are aligned, your products support each other. However, new techniques, new approaches, new technologies can upset the old order and change the relative influence of the complementors or cause the path of fellow travelers to diverge from yours.

These six forces are sketched out in the diagram below.

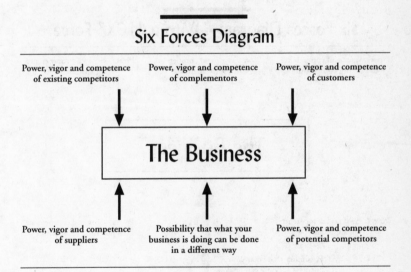

Six Forces Diagram

Power, vigor and competence of existing competitors	Power, vigor and competence of complementors	Power, vigor and competence of customers

The Business

Power, vigor and competence of suppliers	Possibility that what your business is doing can be done in a different way	Power, vigor and competence of potential competitors

When a change in how some element of one's business is conducted becomes an order of magnitude larger than what that business is accustomed to, then all bets are off. There's wind and then there's a typhoon, there are waves and then there's a tsunami. There are competitive forces and then there are supercompetitive forces. I'll call such a very large change in one of these six forces a "10X" change, suggesting that the force has become ten times what it was just recently. This is illustrated in the following diagram.

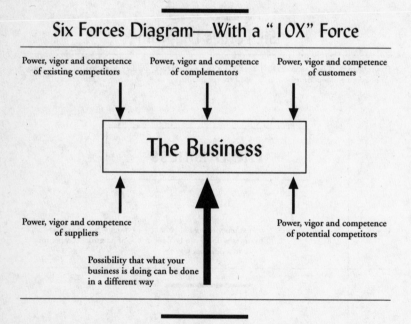

Six Forces Diagram—With a "10X" Force

Power, vigor and competence of existing competitors

Power, vigor and competence of complementors

Power, vigor and competence of customers

The Business

Power, vigor and competence of suppliers

Power, vigor and competence of potential competitors

Possibility that what your business is doing can be done in a different way

When a business goes from the condition shown in the first figure to the second, the changes it faces are enormous. In the face of such "10X" forces, you can lose control of your destiny. Things happen to your business that didn't before, your business no longer responds to your actions as it used to. It is at times like this that the telling phrase "Something has changed" is apt to come up.

To manage a business in the face of a "10X" change is very, very difficult. The business responds differently to managerial actions than it did before. We have lost control and don't know how to regain it. Eventually, a new equilibrium in the industry will be reached. Some businesses will be stronger, others will be weaker. However, the period of transition depicted in the diagram below is particularly confusing and treacherous.

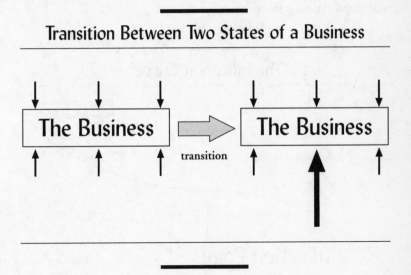

Transition Between Two States of a Business

Now, nobody will ring a bell to call your attention to the fact that you are entering into such a transition. It's a gradual process; the forces start to grow and, as they do, the characteristics of the business begin to change. Only the beginning and the end are clear; the transition in between is gradual and puzzling.

What such a transition does to a business is profound, and how the business manages this transition determines its future. I like to describe this phenomenon as an inflection point.

The Strategic Inflection Point

What is an inflection point? Mathematically, we encounter an inflection point when the rate of change of the slope of the curve (referred to as its "second derivative") changes sign, for instance, going from negative to positive. In physical terms, it's where a curve changes from convex to concave, or vice versa. As shown in the diagram, it's the point at which a curve stops curving one way and starts curving the other way.

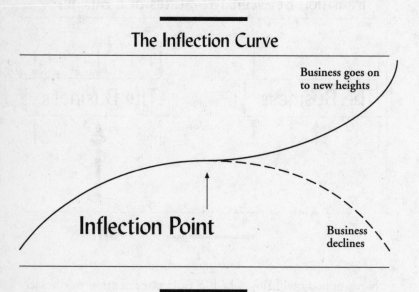

The Inflection Curve

So it is with strategic business matters, too. An inflection point occurs where the old strategic picture dissolves and gives way to the new, allowing the business to ascend to new heights. However, if you don't navigate your way through an inflection point, you go through a peak and after the peak the business declines. It is around such inflection points that managers puzzle and observe, "Things are different. Something has changed."

Put another way, a strategic inflection point is when the balance of forces shifts from the old structure, from the old ways of doing business and the old ways of competing, to the new. Before the strategic inflection point, the industry simply was more like the old. After it, it is more like the new. It is a point where the curve has subtly but profoundly changed, never to change back again.

When exactly does a strategic inflection point take place? It's hard to pinpoint, even in retrospect. Picture yourself going on a hike with a group of friends and getting lost. Some worrywart in the group will be the first one to ask the leader, "Are you sure you know where we're going? Aren't we lost?" The leader will wave him away and march on. But then the uneasiness over lack of trail markers or other familiar signs will grow and at some point the leader will reluctantly stop in his tracks, scratch his head and admit, not too happily, "Hey, guys, I think we *are* lost." The business equivalent of that moment is the strategic inflection point.

But if it's hard to tell in retrospect exactly where a strategic inflection point occurred, how can you tell while going through one? In fact, participants who live through one develop a sense of it being an inflection point at different times, just as the group of hikers suspected they were lost at different moments.

The arguments in the midst of an inflection point can be ferocious. "If our product worked a little better or it cost a little less, we would have no problems," one person will say. And he's probably partially right. "It's just a downturn in the economy. Once capital spending rebounds, we'll resume our growth," another will say. And *he's* probably partially right. Yet another person comes back from a trade show confused and perturbed, and says, "The industry has gone nuts. It's crazy what people use computers for today." He hardly gets a lot of serious attention.

So how do we know that a set of circumstances is a strategic inflection point?

Most of the time, recognition takes place in stages.

First, there is a troubling sense that something is different. Things don't work the way they used to. Customers' attitudes toward you are different. The development groups that have had a history of successes no longer seem to be able to come up with the right product. Competitors that you wrote off or hardly knew existed are stealing business from you. The trade shows seem weird.

Then there is a growing dissonance between what your company thinks it is doing and what is actually happening inside the bowels of the organization. Such misalignment between corporate statements and operational actions hints at more than the normal chaos that you have learned to live with.

Eventually, a new framework, a new set of understandings, a new set of actions emerges. It's as if the group that was lost finds its bearings again. (This could take a year—or a decade.) Last of all, a new set of corporate statements is generated, often by a new set of senior managers.

Perhaps more than getting lost on a hike, working your way through a strategic inflection point is like venturing into what I call the valley of death, the perilous transition between the old and the new ways of doing business. You march in, knowing full well that some of your colleagues will not make it across to the other side. Yet the senior manager's task is to force that march to a vaguely perceived goal in spite of the casualties, and the middle managers' responsibility is to support that decision. There is no other choice.

Ideas about the right direction will split people on the same team. After a while, everyone will understand that the stakes are enormously high. There will be a growing ferocity, determination and seriousness surrounding the views the various participants hold. People will dig in. These divergent views will be held equally strongly, almost like religious tenets. In a workplace that used to function collegially and constructively, holy wars will erupt, pitting coworkers against coworkers, long-term friends against long-term friends. Everything senior management is supposed to do—define direction, set strategies, encourage teamwork, motivate employees—all these things become harder, almost impossible. Everything middle management is supposed to do—implement policy, deal with customers, train employees—also becomes more difficult.

Given the amorphous nature of an inflection point, how do you know the right moment to take appropriate action, to make the changes that will save your company or your career? Unfortunately, you don't.

But you can't wait until you do know: Timing is everything. If you undertake these changes while your company is still healthy, while your ongoing business forms a protective bubble in which you can experiment with the new ways of doing business, you can save much more of your company's strength, your employees and your strategic position. But that means acting when not everything is known, when the data aren't yet in. Even those who believe in a scientific approach to management will have to rely on instinct and personal judgment. When you're caught in the turbulence of a strategic inflection point, the sad fact is that instinct and judgment are all you've got to guide you through.

But the good news is that even though your judgment got you into this tough position, it can also get you out. It's just a question of training your instincts to pick up a different set of signals. These signals may have been out there all along but you may have ignored them. The strategic inflection point is the time to wake up and listen.

The Morphing of the Computer Industry

''Not only has the basis of computing changed, the basis of competition has changed too.''

O f all the changes in the forces of competition, the most difficult one to deal with is when one of the forces becomes so strong that it transforms the very essence of how business is conducted in an industry. There are plenty of historic examples, such as how railroads revolutionized transportation, and many contemporary ones, such as how small retailers are being wiped out by superstores. The lessons and the dynamics of what happens seem to be the same, no matter what the industry, no matter where it is located and no matter which era it operates in.

I would like to describe how this all works by going in detail through an example that's close to my heart. When computers could be built around a simple commonly available microprocessor and, consequently, the personal computer appeared on the scene, it brought with it a cost-effectiveness that was easily ten times greater than was available with the type of computing that preceded it. In a little over five years, the cost adjusted by performance decreased by 90 percent, an unprecedented rate of decline. Such an enormous change in the way computing could be done had profound consequences on the computing business.

Before the Strategic Inflection Point

The computer industry used to be vertically aligned. As shown in the diagram that follows, this means that an old-style computer company would have its own semiconductor chip implementation, build its own computer around these chips according to its own design and in its own factories, develop its own operating system software (the software that is fundamental to the workings of all computers) and market its own applications software (the software that does things like accounts payable or airline ticketing or department store inventory control). This combination of a company's own chips, own computers, own operating systems and own applications software would then be sold as a package by the company's own salespeople. This is what we mean by a vertical alignment. Note how often the word "own" occurs in this description. In fact, we might as well say "proprietary," which, in fact, was the byword of the old computer industry.

The Old Vertical Computer Industry— Circa 1980

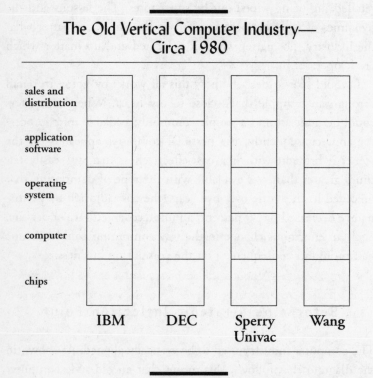

	IBM	DEC	Sperry Univac	Wang
sales and distribution				
application software				
operating system				
computer				
chips				

A company competed in this industry as one vertical proprietary block against all other computer companies' vertical proprietary blocks. Salesmen would show up and offer their vertical combination of things, and the company they were selling to would decide to buy one proprietary line and not the others.

This arrangement had its pluses and minuses. The pluses were that, when a company developed its own chips, its own hardware and its own software, sold and serviced by its own people, all the parts would be made to work together as a seamless total. The minuses were that, once you bought into this proprietary arrangement, you were stuck with it. If there was a problem, you couldn't throw out just one part of the vertical stack; you would have to abandon the entire stack, and that was a big deal. So customers of vertical computer companies tended to stay for a long time with the solution they chose in the first place. Needless to say, competition for the first sale was ferocious in the extreme, because whoever won that sale had the long-term advantage. This was how business was done for decades.

Then the microprocessor appeared, followed by the "10X" force of the personal computer built on it. The "10X" force came about because technology now permitted putting what before had been many chips on one single chip and because the same microprocessor could be used to produce all kinds of personal computers. As the microprocessor became the basic building block of the industry, the economics of mass production kicked in and manufacturing computers became extremely cost-effective, making the PC an enormously attractive tool in both home and business settings.

Over time, this changed the entire structure of the industry and a new horizontal industry emerged. In this new model, no one company had its own stack. A consumer could pick a chip from the horizontal chip bar, pick a computer manufacturer from the computer bar, choose an operating system out of the operating system bar, grab one of several ready-to-use applications off the shelf at a retail store or at a computer superstore and take the collection of these things home. Then he or she fired them up and hoped that they would all work together. He might have trouble making them work but he put up with that trouble and worked a bit harder because for $2,000 he had just bought a computer system that the old way couldn't deliver for less than ten times the cost. This was such a compelling proposition that he put up with the weaknesses in order to avail himself of the power of this new way of doing business. Over time, this changed the entire structure of the computer industry, and a new horizontal industry, depicted below, emerged.

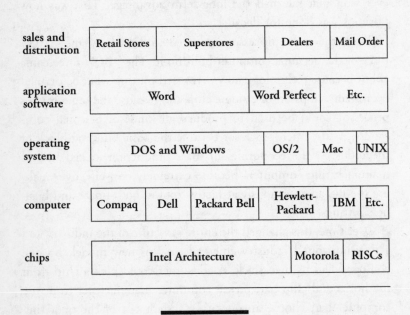

The New Horizontal Computer Industry— Circa 1995
(not to scale)

sales and distribution	Retail Stores	Superstores		Dealers	Mail Order
application software	Word			Word Perfect	Etc.
operating system	DOS and Windows			OS/2	Mac · UNIX
computer	Compaq · Dell · Packard Bell			Hewlett-Packard	IBM · Etc.
chips	Intel Architecture				Motorola · RISCs

In this diagram, we have horizontal bars representing fields of both competence and competition. In chips, suppliers of microprocessors using the Intel microprocessor architecture compete with companies such as Motorola and others who supply different types of microprocessors. In computers, a basic computer design is supplied by a variety of computer manufacturers, such as Compaq, IBM, Packard Bell, Dell and many others. These computers are fundamentally similar even if the computer company engineers improve the basic machine as they compete with each other.

In operating systems, again, there are a few well-established types. Over most of the decade of the eighties, Microsoft's early operating system, DOS, prevailed. In the nineties, this was modified to become easier to use and Windows emerged, which competes with IBM's OS/2, Apple's Mac OS and a number of UNIX-based operating systems.

A visit to a neighborhood computer store shows all sorts of applications software competing for shelf space as well as for customers: spreadsheets, word processing, database packages, calendar software and the like. Sales and distribution of computer products have also become enormously eclectic. Retail stores compete with dealers who compete with superstores. Each of these carries a number of manufacturers' computers and software vendors' products, just as many grocery stores carry different brands of toothpaste.

So, throughout the decade of the eighties, the way computing was done changed, from the old vertical way to the new horizontal way. First individuals using computers changed to PCs, then big-time computing increasingly started to be done this way. Over time, the entire structure of the industry metamorphosed to a horizontal structure, as shown on the next page.

Even in retrospect, I can't put my finger on exactly where the inflection point took place in the computer industry. Was it in the

The Transformation of the Computer Industry

(not to scale)

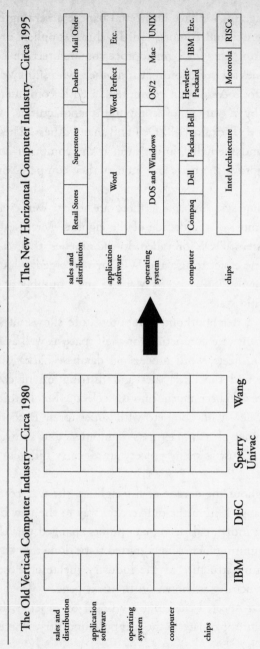

early eighties, when PCs started to emerge? Was it in the second half of the decade, when networks based on PC technology started to grow in number? It's hard to say. But some facts are clear: Going into the eighties, the old computer companies were strong, vital and growing. IBM projected that they would be a $100 billion company by the end of the decade. But by the end of the 1980s, many large vertical computer companies were in the midst of layoffs and restructuring, and a whole new set of players emerged. I keep thinking of a computer-generated image of a person "morphing" from one face to another, one face imperceptibly dissolving and another simultaneously taking shape. You can't tell the precise point when the first face disappears and the new face replaces it. You only know that at the beginning of the process you have one face and at the end of the process you have another face, but you can't identify any point where the image is any more one than the other. So it was here, even in retrospect.

As this transformation progressed, companies that had become prosperous in the old vertical computer industry found their lives increasingly difficult. But at the same time, the new order provided an opportunity for a number of new entries to shoot into preeminence. Compaq became the fastest Fortune 500 company to reach $1 billion in revenue. They were a company that understood the dynamics of the new industry and prospered by tailoring their business model to it. So did many others, like Dell and Novell. More about these later.

After the Strategic Inflection Point

Not only had the basis of computing changed, the basis of competition had changed too. Competitors in each horizontal bar of competence and competition now fought for the largest share of that bar. The power of this approach to computing is based on mass production and mass distribution. Those that win inevitably get stronger; those that lose, over time, get weaker.

After 1981, when IBM chose Intel to provide the microprocessor in their PC, Intel grew to become the most widely accepted supplier of microprocessors. After that, industry participants in the layers above, i.e., computer manufacturers and operating systems suppliers, found it more economically advantageous to build their business on Intel architecture microchips than on any other. Why? Because there were a lot more of those being produced every year. If you base your business on the volume leader, you will be going after a larger business yourself.

Developers of applications programs were driven toward volume as well. Their alternatives were to develop a product based on Microsoft's market-share-leading Windows or on competitive operating systems with a smaller market share. Over time, they chose to base their work on the former, gradually reinforcing the success of Intel's microprocessors and Microsoft's operating systems.

The transformation of the industry from the old model to the new didn't take place in one instant. It took place over years. It took place in many small steps—as mainframe computers lost new applications to PCs, as programmers shifted their attention, as old software companies shrank and new software companies grew. Over time, thousands of such individual events made up the transformation.

Let's think about what this transformation from the vertical industry structure to the horizontal must have been like at one of the mainframe computer companies. In particular, let's look at it from IBM's standpoint. IBM had been the strongest player in the old industry. What was the impact of this change on IBM?

First of all, IBM's growth slowed down as much of computing went from mainframes to microprocessor-based personal computers. But that's not all. IBM was composed of a group of people who had won time and time again, decade after decade, in the battle among vertical computer players. The managers who ran IBM grew up in this world. They got selected for their excellence in developing products and competing in the marketplace within this framework. Their long reign of success deeply reinforced and ingrained the thought processes and instincts that led to winning in the vertical industry. So when the industry changed, they attempted to use the same type of thinking regarding product development and competitiveness that had worked so well in the past.

Even something as simple as the choice of the name "OS/2" showed how IBM missed the significance of the horizontal industry. The idea of OS/2, a new personal computer operating system, was introduced in 1987 at the same time as a new line of IBM personal computers called the "PS/2." Even though it wasn't necessarily the case, the inference was that OS/2 worked only on PS/2 computers. That perception alone might have been enough to limit the success of OS/2, since the majority of personal computers were made by IBM's competitors, not by IBM itself.

But there was, in fact, more to it than just that. It took a long while before IBM actually provided the necessary adaptations to OS/2 to make it work with other manufacturers' computers and an even longer time before IBM started marketing their operating systems to other computer manufacturers—their competitors—so that those manufacturers could ship OS/2 with their computers as they were accustomed to doing with DOS and Windows.

I happened to be a witness as an IBM manager who was involved with both the PS/2 line of personal computers and the OS/2 operating system tried to persuade another large personal computer manufacturer to adopt OS/2 for the latter's PC line. It was the oddest marketing meeting ever. These two people thought of themselves, first and foremost, as PC competitors. Even though his primary mission was to popularize OS/2, the IBM person was emotionally hamstrung in his attempt to market to his competitor. At the same time, the representative of the other computer

manufacturer was reluctant to rely on IBM—a PC competitor—
for such an important piece of technology as the operating system. The conversation was awkward and tense; the deal never
materialized. OS/2 still hasn't gained broad popularity in the industry.

Clearly, the old world was no more. Something had changed.
And the more successful the players were in the earlier industry,
the harder a time they had to change with it.

Winners and Losers

When an industry goes through a strategic inflection point, the
practitioners of the old art may have trouble. On the other hand,
the new landscape provides an opportunity for people, some of
whom may not even be participants in the industry in question,
to join and become part of the action.

I have mentioned Compaq as an example of a computer company that skyrocketed by becoming a practitioner of the new
horizontal computer industry. Although their original business
model consisted of being a follower of IBM as a maker of IBM-
compatible personal computers, when the introduction of a new
microprocessor in 1985 provided an opportunity to go for a market-share-leading position, they took the chance and got out in
front, ahead of IBM. This initiative propelled them to a growing
share of the PC bar and eventually they even passed IBM as the
world's largest maker of IBM-compatible PCs.

There were others who, being born into the new order, were
unfettered by old concepts or old rules. In the early eighties,
Michael Dell started supplying his friends with computers he
assembled out of parts in his dorm room at the University of
Texas. Basically, he tapped into the desire of customers of the
horizontal PC industry for low-cost standard computer systems.
Later, Dell built on his experience and started a company based

on the premise that people other than his college friends would also be interested in purchasing computers customized to their specific needs and supplied through direct means—in this case, through orders taken over the phone, with computers delivered by parcel post. No member of the old computer industry would have given a chance to a proposition that said that people would buy computers through the mail. It would simply have been seen as an unnatural act: just as dogs don't fly, people don't buy mail-order computers. At least, they didn't in the old world order.

Today, Dell Computer Corporation of Austin, Texas, is doing about $5 billion worth of business a year, still true to its original premise—selling personal computers custom-assembled to the individual buyer's specifications, through the mail. This could only happen in a world of computers that is characterized by low-cost, mass-produced, mass-consumed items.

Few of the top ten participants in the new horizontal computer industry rose from the ranks of the old vertical computer industry, bearing testimony to the observation that it is truly difficult for a successful industry participant to adapt to a completely different industry structure.

Some members of the old industry managed to renew themselves in a manner that was consistent with the new industry structure but would not have been with the old. NCR, in the early eighties, before the transition gathered speed, was one of the bigger vertical computer players. It was among the first, if not *the* first, to recognize the forces of change. Over the course of a few years (and before they were acquired by AT&T), NCR moved their entire computer line onto commonly available microprocessors. They abandoned their proprietary chips and hardware design, and made major modifications in their software, so that what was originally designed to run on their proprietary architecture would now run on off-the-shelf microprocessors.

Unisys, a vertical computer company created from the combination of two independent computer companies, Sperry and Burroughs, was another one of the players in the old computer industry, a multibillion-dollar company. They hit hard times as the strategic inflection point wreaked havoc on the vertical companies. In adapting, Unisys, once a proud designer of first-class computers, moved their strategic focus to software and services built around the products of the new horizontal computer industry. In effect, they came to the conclusion that they couldn't fight this industry-wide change, so they adapted to it.

Sometimes the changes are even more dramatic. In the early eighties, Novell was a small company fashioned along the lines of the old computer industry. They built hardware and developed network software to run on their own hardware. They, too, hit hard times. Novell's then head, Ray Noorda, often tells the story that it wasn't very hard to figure out what to do. They simply didn't have enough money to continue to pay their suppliers, so they abandoned their hardware business and concentrated on software where they didn't need to worry about supplier bills. Then they moved their software onto inexpensive standard PCs. By moving quickly into a new way of doing business, Novell became a "first mover" in networking in the new horizontal industry and became a billion-dollar software company by the end of the decade.

There is an important lesson to be learned from Novell's experience. Whereas as a hardware producer Novell had lack of scale working *against* them, by being the first to popularize networking software that runs on PCs and capturing a large share of the emerging networking market, they made scale work *for* them. They turned from losers to winners.

In fact, there are two more lessons here. First, when a strategic inflection point sweeps through the industry, the more successful a participant was in the old industry structure, the more threatened it is by change and the more reluctant it is to adapt to it. Second, whereas the cost to enter a given industry in the face of well-entrenched participants can be very high, when the structure breaks, the cost to enter may become trivially small, giving rise to Compaqs, Dells and Novells, each of which emerged from practically nothing to become major corporations. What's common among these companies is that they all instinctively followed the rules for success in a horizontal industry.

The New Rules of the Horizontal Industry

Horizontal industries live and die by mass production and mass marketing. They have their own rules. The companies that have done well in the brutally competitive horizontal computer industry have learned these implicit rules. By following them, a company has the opportunity to compete and prosper. By defying them, no matter how good its products are, no matter how well they execute their plans, a company is slogging uphill.

What are these rules? There are three.

One, don't differentiate without a difference. Don't introduce improvements whose only purpose is to give you an advantage over your competitor without giving your customer a substantial advantage. The personal computer industry is characterized by well-chronicled failures when manufacturers, ostensibly motivated by a desire to make "a better PC," departed from the mainstream standard. But goodness in a PC was inseparable from compatibility, so "a better PC" that was different turned out to be a technological oxymoron.

Two, in this hypercompetitive horizontal world, opportunity knocks when a technology break or other fundamental change comes your way. Grab it. The first mover and only the first mover, the company that acts while the others dither, has a true opportunity to gain time over its competitors—and time advantage, in this business, is the surest way to gain market share.

Conversely, people who try to fight the wave of a new technology lose in spite of their best efforts because they waste valuable time.

Three, price for what the market will bear, price for volume, then work like the devil on your costs so that you can make money at that price. This will lead you to achieve economies of scale in which the large investments that are necessary can be effective and productive and will make sense because, by being a large-volume supplier, you can spread and recoup those costs. By contrast, cost-based pricing will often lead you into a niche position, which in a mass-production-based industry is not very lucrative.

I think these rules are pretty general for horizontally based industries. I also think that there is a general trend toward horizontally based structure in many parts of industry and commerce: As an industry becomes more competitive, companies are forced to retreat to their strongholds and specialize, in order to become world class in whatever segment they end up occupying.

Why is this so?

In our example, a vertical computer company had to produce computer platforms *and* operating systems *and* software. A horizontal computer company, however, supplies just one product— for example, computer platforms *or* operating systems *or* software. By virtue of the functional specialization that prevails, horizontal industries tend to be more cost-effective than their vertical equivalents. Simply put, it's harder to be the best of class in several fields than in just one.

As industries shift from the vertical to the horizontal model, each participant will have to work its way through a strategic inflection point. Consequently, operating by these rules will be necessary for a larger and larger class of companies as time goes on.

4

They're Everywhere

''Strategic inflection points are not a phenomenon of the high-tech industry, nor are they something that happens to the other guy.''

W hen a Wal-Mart moves into a small town, the environment changes for every retailer in that town. A "10X" factor has arrived. When the technology for sound in movies became popular, every silent actor and actress personally experienced the "10X" factor of technological change. When container shipping revolutionized sea transportation, a "10X" factor reordered the major ports around the world.

Reading the daily newspapers through a "10X" lens constantly exposes potential strategic inflection points. Does the wave of bank mergers that is sweeping the United States today have anything to do with a "10X" change? Does the acquisition of ABC by Disney or Time Warner's proposed merger with Turner Broadcasting System have anything to do with one? Does the self-imposed breakup of AT&T?

In subsequent chapters, I will discuss common reactions and behavior that occur when strategic inflection points arise, as well as approaches and techniques for dealing with them. My purpose in this chapter is to sweep through a variety of examples of strategic inflection points drawn from different industries. By learning from the painful experience of others, we can improve our ability to recognize a strategic inflection point that's about to affect us. And that's half the battle.

I'll largely use the framework of Porter's competitive analysis model, as most strategic inflection points originate with a large "10X" change in one of the forces affecting the business. I will describe examples that are triggered by a "10X" change in the force of the competition, a "10X" change in the technology, a "10X" change in the power of customers, a "10X" change in the power of suppliers and complementors, and a "10X" change that is due to the imposition or the removal of regulations. The pervasiveness of the "10X" factor raises the question, "Is every strategic inflection point characterized by a '10X' change? And does every '10X' change lead to a strategic inflection point?" I think for all practical purposes the answer to both of these questions is yes.

"10 X" Change: Competition

There's competition and there's megacompetition, and when there's megacompetition—a "10X" force—the business landscape changes. Sometimes the nature of the megacompetition is obvious, and the story of Wal-Mart that follows will give an example of that. Sometimes the megacompetition sneaks up on you. It doesn't do business the way you are used to having business done, but it will lure your customers away just the same. The story of Next will give an example of that.

Wal-Mart: An overwhelming force in town

From the standpoint of a general store in a small town, a Wal-Mart store is competition. So were the other general stores that it previously had to compete with. But Wal-Mart comes to town with a superior "just-in-time" logistics system, with inventory management based on modern scanners and satellite communications; with trucks that go from store to hub to store continuously replenishing inventories; with large-volume-based purchase costs, systematic companywide training programs, and a finely tuned store location system designed to pinpoint areas where competition is generally weak. All this adds up to a "10X" factor compared to the other competition the store previously had to face. For a small-town general store, once Wal-Mart moves to town, things will have changed in a big way.

A far superior competitor appearing on the scene is a mandate for you to change. Continuing to do what worked before doesn't work anymore.

What would work against a Wal-Mart? Specialization has a good chance. In-depth stocking, serving a particular market segment, as Home Depot, Office Depot, Toys "Я" Us and similar "category killers" are doing, can work to offset the overall imbalance of scale. So can customized service, as Staples is implementing through an in-depth computerized customer database. Alternatively, so might redefining your business to provide an environment, rather than a product, that people value, like the example of an independent bookstore that became a coffeehouse with books to compete with the chain bookstores that brought Wal-Mart-style competitive advantages to their business.

Next: The software company

When Steve Jobs cofounded Apple, he created an immensely successful, fully vertical personal computer company. Apple made their own hardware, designed their own operating system software, and created their own graphical user interface (what the customer sees on the computer screen when he or she starts working with the computer). They even attempted to develop their own applications.

When Jobs left Apple in 1985, he set out, for all intents and purposes, to recreate the same success story. He just wanted to do it better. As even the name of his new company implied, he wanted to create the "Next" generation of superbly engineered hardware, a graphical user interface that was even better than Apple's Macintosh interface and an operating system that was capable of more advanced tasks than the Mac. The software would be built in such a way that customers could tailor applications to their own uses by rearranging chunks of existing software rather than having to write it from the ground up.

Jobs wanted to tie all of this—the hardware, the basic software and the graphical user interface—together to create a computer system that would be in a class by itself. It took a few years, but he did something close to that. The Next computer and operating system delivered on basically all of these objectives.

Yet while Jobs was focusing on an ambitious and complex development task, he ignored a key development that was to render most of his efforts futile. While he and his employees were spending days and nights developing the superb sleek computer, a mass-produced, broadly available graphical user interface, Microsoft Windows, had come on the market. Windows wasn't even as good as the Mac, let alone the Next interface, and it wasn't seamlessly integrated with computers or applications. But it was cheap, it worked and, most importantly, it worked on the inexpensive and increasingly powerful personal computers that by the late eighties were available from hundreds of PC manufacturers.

While Jobs was burning the midnight oil inside Next, in the outside world something changed.

When Jobs started developing Next, the competition he had in mind was the Mac. PCs were not even a blip on his competitive radar screen. After all, at that time PCs didn't even have an easy-to-use graphical interface.

But by the time the Next computer system emerged three years later, Microsoft's persistent efforts with Windows were about to change the PC environment. The world of Windows would share some of the characteristics of the Mac world in that it provided a graphical user interface, but it also retained the fundamental characteristics of the PC world, i.e., Windows worked on computers that were available anywhere in the world from hundreds of sources. As a result of fierce competition by the hundreds of computer manufacturers supplying them, these computers became far more affordable than the Mac.

It was as if Steve Jobs and his company had gone into a time capsule when they started Next. They worked hard for years, competing against what they thought was the competition, but by the time they emerged, the competition turned out to be something completely different and much more powerful. Although they were oblivious to it, Next found itself in the midst of a strategic inflection point.

The Next machine never took off. In fact, despite ongoing infusions of investors' cash, Next was hemorrhaging money. They were trying to maintain an expensive computer development operation, in addition to a state-of-the-art software development operation, plus a fully automated factory built to produce a large volume of Next computers—a large volume that never materialized. By 1991, about six years after its founding, Next was in financial difficulties.

Some managers inside the company had advocated throwing in the towel in hardware and porting their crown jewel to mass-produced PCs. Jobs resisted this for a long time. He didn't like PCs. He thought they were inelegant and poorly engineered, and the many players in the industry made any kind of uniformity hard to achieve. In short, Jobs thought PCs were a mess. The thing is, he was right. But what Jobs missed at the time was that the very messiness of the PC industry that he despised was the result of its power: many companies competing to offer better value to ever larger numbers of customers.

Some of his managers got frustrated and quit, yet their idea continued to ferment. As Next's funds grew lower and lower, Jobs finally accepted the inevitability of the inelegant, messy PC industry as his environment. He threw his weight behind the proposal he had fought. He shut down all hardware development and the spanking new automated factory, and laid off half of his staff.

Bowing to the "10X" force of the PC industry, Next, the software company, was born.

Steve Jobs is arguably the founding genius of the personal computer industry, the person who at age twenty saw what in the next decade would become a $100 billion worldwide industry. Yet ten years later, at thirty, Jobs was stuck in his own past. In his past, "insanely great computers," a favorite phrase of his, won in the market. Graphical interfaces were powerful differentiators because PC software was clunky. As things changed, although many of his managers knew better, Jobs did not easily give up the conviction that had made him such a passionate and effective pioneer. It took facing a business survival situation for reality to win over long-held dogmas.

"10 X" Change: Technology

Technology changes all the time. Typewriters get better, cars get better, computers get better. Most of this change is gradual: Competitors deliver the next improvement, we respond, they respond in turn and so it goes. However, every once in a while, technology changes in a dramatic way. Something can be done that could not be done before, or something can be done "10X" better, faster or cheaper than it would have been done before.

We'll look at a few examples that are clear because they are in the past. But even as I write this, technological developments are brewing that are likely to bring changes of the same magnitude—or bigger—in the years ahead. Will digital entertainment replace movies as we know them? Will digital information replace newspapers and magazines? Will remote banking render conventional banks relics of the past? Will the wider availability of interconnected computers bring wholesale changes to the practice of medicine?

To be sure, not all technological possibilities have a major impact. Electric cars haven't, nor has commercial nuclear power generation. But some have and others will.

Sound takes over silent movies

"Something changed" when *The Jazz Singer* debuted on October 6, 1927. Movies didn't used to have sound; now they did. With that single qualitative change, the lives of many stars and many directors of the silent movies were affected in a profound way. Some made the change, while some tried to adapt and failed. Others still clung to their old trade, simply adopting an attitude of denial in the face of a major environmental change and rationalizing their actions by questioning why anyone would want talking movies.

As late as 1931, Charlie Chaplin was still fighting the move to sound. In an interview that year, he proclaimed, "I give the talkies six months more." Chaplin's powerful audience appeal and craftsmanship were such that he was able to make successful silent movies throughout the 1930s. However, even Charlie Chaplin couldn't hold out forever. Chaplin finally surrendered to spoken dialogue with *The Great Dictator* in 1940.

Others adjusted with great agility. Greta Garbo was a superstar of silent movies. With the advent of sound, in 1930 her studio introduced her to speaking roles in *Anna Christie*. Billboards proclaiming "Garbo speaks!" advertised the movie across the country. The movie was both a critical and a commercial success and Garbo went on to establish herself as a star of silent films who made a successful transition to talkies. What company would not be envious of getting through a strategic inflection point with such alacrity?

Yet is this industry going to be equally successful in navigating another strategic inflection point that's caused by the advent of digital technology, by which actors can be replaced by lifelike-looking, live-sounding digital creations? Pixar's movie *Toy Story* is an example of what could be done in this fashion. It's the first feature-length result of a new technology. What will this technology be able to do three years from now, five years from now, ten years from now? I suspect this technology will bring with it another strategic inflection point. It never ends.

Upheaval in the shipping industry

Technology transformed the worldwide shipping industry as dramatically and decisively as sound transformed the movie industry. In the span of a decade, a virtual instant in the history of shipping, the standardization of shipbuilding designs, the creation of refrigerated transport ships and, most importantly, the evolution of containerization—a technology that permitted the easy transfer of cargo on and off ships—introduced a "10X" change in the productivity of shipping, reversing an inexorably rising trend in costs. The situation was ripe for a technological breakthrough in the way ports handled cargo—and it came.

As with the movie industry, some ports made the change, others tried but couldn't, and many resolutely fought this trend. Consequently, the new technologies led to a worldwide reordering of shipping ports. As of the time of this writing, Singapore, its skyline filled with the silhouettes of modern port equipment, has emerged as a major shipping center in Southeast Asia and Seattle has become one of the foremost ports for containerized cargo ships on the West Coast. Without the room to accommodate modern equipment, New York City, once a major magnet for shipping, has been steadily losing money. Ports that didn't adopt the new technologies have become candidates for redevelopment into shopping malls, recreation areas and waterfront apartment complexes.

After each strategic inflection point, there are winners and there are losers. Whether a port won or lost clearly depended on how it responded to the "10X" force in technology that engulfed it.

A fundamental rule in technology says that whatever *can* be done *will* be done. Consequently, once the PC brought a "10X" lower cost for a given performance, it was only a matter of time before its impact would spread through the entire computing world and transform it. This change didn't happen from one day to the next. It came gradually, as the graph below indicates with price/performance trends.

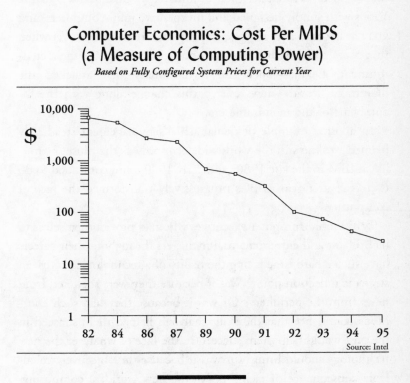

Computer Economics: Cost Per MIPS (a Measure of Computing Power)
Based on Fully Configured System Prices for Current Year

Source: Intel

There were people in the industry who could surmise the appearance of this trend and who concluded that the price/performance characteristics of microprocessor-based PCs would win out in time. Some companies—NCR and Hewlett-Packard come to mind—modified their strategies to take advantage of the power of microprocessors. Other companies were in denial, much as Chaplin was with talkies.

Denial took different forms. In 1984 the then head of Digital Equipment Corporation, the largest mini-computer maker at the time, sounding a lot like Chaplin, described PCs as "cheap, short-lived and not-very-accurate machines." This attitude was especially ironic when you consider Digital's past. Digital broke into the world of computers, then dominated by mainframes, in the 1960s with simply designed and inexpensive mini-computers, and grew to become a very large company with that strategy. Yet when they were faced with a new technological change in their environment, Digital—once the revolutionary that attacked the mainframe world—now resisted this change along with the incumbents of the mainframe era.

In another example of denial, IBM's management steadfastly blamed weakness in the worldwide economy as the cause of trouble at IBM in the late 1980s and early 1990s, and continued to do that year after year as PCs progressively transformed the face of computing.

Why would computer executives who had proven themselves to be brilliant and entrepreneurial managers throughout their careers have such a hard time facing the reality of a technologically driven strategic inflection point? Was it because they were sheltered from news from the periphery? Or was it because they had such enormous confidence that the skills that had helped them succeed in the past would help them succeed in the face of whatever the new technology should bring? Or was it because the objectively calculable consequence of facing up to the new world of computing, like the monumental cutbacks in staff that would be necessary, were so painful as to be inconceivable? It's hard to know but the reaction is all too common. I think all these factors played a part, but the last one—the resistance to facing a painful new world— was the most important.

Perhaps the best analogy to Charlie Chaplin's late conversion to the new medium is recent reports that Steve Chen, the former key designer of the immensely succesful Cray supercomputers, started a company of his own based on high-performance, industry-standard microprocessor chips. Chen's previous company, which attempted to create the world's fastest supercomputer, was one of the last holdouts of the old computing paradigm. But as Chen described his switch to a technological approach he once eschewed, he did so with a slight understatement: "I took a different approach this time."

"10 X" Change: Customers

Customers drifting away from their former buying habits may provide the most subtle and insidious cause of a strategic inflection point—subtle and insidious because it takes place slowly. In an analysis of the history of business failures, Harvard Business School Professor Richard Tedlow came to the conclusion that businesses fail either because they leave their customers, i.e., they arbitrarily change a strategy that worked for them in the past (the obvious change), or because their customers leave them (the subtle one).

Think about it: Right now, a whole generation of young people in the United States has been brought up to take computers for granted. Pointing with a mouse is no more mysterious to them than hitting the "on" button on the television is to their parents. They feel utterly comfortable with using computers and are no more affected by their computer crashing than their parents are when their car stalls on a cold morning: They just shrug, mumble something and start up again. When they go to college, these young people get their homework assignments on the college's networked computers, do their research on the Internet and arrange their weekend activities by e-mail.

Consumer companies that are counting on these young people as future customers need to be concerned with the pervasive change in how they get and generate information, transact their business and live their lives, or else those companies may lose their customers' attention. Doesn't this represent a demographic time bomb that is ticking away?

Changing tastes in cars

None of this is new. During the 1920s the market for automobiles changed slowly and subtly. Henry Ford's slogan for the Model T—"It takes you there and brings you back"—epitomized the original attraction of the car as a mode of basic transportation. In 1921, more than half of all cars sold in the United States were Fords. But in a post-World War I world in which style and leisure had become important considerations in people's lives, Alfred Sloan at General Motors saw a market for "a car for every purse and purpose." Thanks to GM's introduction of a varied product line and annual model changes, by the end of the decade General Motors had taken the lead in both profits and market share, and would continue to outperform Ford in profit for more than sixty years. General Motors saw the market changing and went with the change.

Attitude shifts

Sometimes a change in the customer base represents a subtle change of attitude, yet one so inexorable that it can have a "10X" force. In hindsight, the consumer reaction to the Pentium processor's floating point flaw in 1994 represented such a change. The center of gravity of Intel's customer base shifted over time from the computer manufacturers to the computer users. The "Intel

Inside" program begun in 1991 established a mindset in computer users that they were, in fact, Intel's customers, even though they didn't actually buy anything from us. It was an attitude change, a change we actually stimulated, but one whose impact we at Intel did not fully comprehend.

Is the Pentium processor floating point incident a stand-alone incident, a bump in the road or, to use electronic parlance, "noise"? Or is it a "signal," a fundamental change in whom we sell to and whom we service? I think it is the latter. The computer industry has largely become one that services consumers who use their own discretionary spending to purchase a product, and who apply the same expectations to those products that they have for other household goods. Intel has had to start adjusting to this new reality, and so have other players in this industry. The environment has changed for all of us. The good news is, we all have a much larger market. The bad news is, it is a much tougher market than we were accustomed to servicing.

The point is, what is a demographic time bomb for consumer companies represents good news for us in the computer business. Millions of young people grow up computer-savvy, taking our products for granted as a part of their lives. But (and there is always a but!) they're going to be a lot more demanding of a product, a lot more discerning of weaknesses in it. Are all of us in this industry getting ready for this subtle shift? I'm not so sure.

The double whammy in supercomputers

Sometimes more than one of the six competitive forces changes in a big way. The combination of factors results in a strategic inflection point that can be even more dramatic than a strategic inflection point caused by just one force. The supercomputer industry, the part of the computer industry that supplies the most powerful of all computers, provides a good case in point. Supercomputers are used to study everything from nuclear energy to weather patterns. The industry's approach was similar to the old vertical computer industry. Its customer base was heavily dependent on government spending, defense projects and other types of "Big Research."

Both changed in approximately the same time frame. Technology moved to a microprocessor base and government spending dried up when the Cold War ended, increasing pressure on defense-spending reduction. The result is that a $1 billion industry that had been the pride and joy of U.S. technology and a mainstay of the defense posture of this country is suddenly in trouble. Nothing signifies this more than the fact that Cray Computer Corporation, a company founded by the icon of the supercomputer age, Seymour Cray, was unable to maintain operations due to lack of funds. It's yet another example illustrating that the person who is the star of a previous era is often the last one to adapt to change, the last one to yield to the logic of a strategic inflection point and tends to fall harder than most.

"10X" Change: Suppliers

Businesses often take their suppliers for granted. They are there to serve us and, if we don't like what they do, we tend to think we can always replace them with someone who better fills our needs. But sometimes, whether because of a change in technology or a change in industry structure, suppliers can become very powerful—so powerful, in fact, that they can affect the way the rest of the industry does business.

Airlines flex their muscles

Recently, the supplier base in the travel industry has attempted to flex its muscles. Here, the principal supplier is the airlines, which used to grant travel agents a 10 percent commission on every ticket sold. Even though travel-agent commissions were the airline industry's third largest cost (after labor and fuel), airlines had avoided changing the commission rates because travel agents sell about 85 percent of all tickets and they did not want to antagonize them. However, rising prices and industry cutbacks finally forced the airlines to place a cap on commissions.

Can travel agencies continue as before in the face of a significant loss of income? Within days of the airlines' decision, two of the country's largest agencies instituted a policy of charging customers for low-cost purchases. Will such a charge stick? What should the travel agencies do if the caps on commissions remain a fact of life and if their customers won't absorb any of their changes? One industry association predicted that 40 percent of all agencies might go out of business. It is possible that this single act by the suppliers can precipitate a strategic inflection point that might in time alter the entire travel industry.

The end of second sourcing

Intel, in its capacity as a supplier of microprocessors, accelerated the morphing of the computer industry when we changed our practice of second sourcing.

Second sourcing, once common in our industry, refers to a practice in which a supplier, in order to make sure that his product is widely accepted, turns to his competitors and offers them technical know-how, so that they, too, can supply this product.

In theory, this unnatural competitive act works out as a win for all parties: the developer of the product benefits by a wider customer acceptance of the product as a result of a broader supplier base; the second-source supplier, who is a recipient of the technology, clearly benefits by getting valuable technology while giving little in return. And the customer for the product in question benefits by having a larger number of suppliers who will compete for his business.

In practice, however, things don't often work out that well. When the product needs help in the marketplace, the second source usually is not yet producing, so the primary source and the customers don't have the benefit of the extended supply. Once the product is fully in production and supply catches up with demand, the second source is in production too, so multiple companies now compete for the same business. This may please the customer but certainly hurts the wallet of the prime source. And so it goes.

By the mid-eighties, we found that the disadvantages of this practice outweighed its advantages for us. So we changed. Our resolve hardened by tough business conditions (more about this in the next chapter), we decided to demand tangible compensation for our technology.

Our competitors were reluctant to pay for technology that we used to give away practically for free. Consequently, in the transition to the next microprocessor generation, we ended up with no second source and became the only source of microprocessors to our customers. Eventually our competition stopped waiting for our largesse and developed similar products on their own, but this took a number of years.

The impact this relatively minor change had on the entire PC industry was enormous. A key commodity, the standard microprocessor on which most personal computers were built, became available only from its developer—us. This, in turn, had two consequences. First, our influence on our customers increased. From their standpoint, this might have appeared as a "10X" force. Second, since most PCs increasingly were built on microprocessors from one supplier, they became more alike. This, in turn, had an impact on software developers, who could now concentrate their efforts on developing software for fundamentally similar computers built by many manufacturers. The result of the morphing of the computer industry, i.e., the emergence of computers as a practically interchangeable commodity, has been greatly aided by the common microprocessor on which they were built.

"10X" Change: Complementors

Changes in technology affecting the business of your complementors, companies whose products you depend on, can also have a profound effect on your business. The personal computer industry and Intel have had a mutual dependence on personal computing software companies. Should major technological changes affect the software business, through the complementary relationship these changes might affect our business as well.

For example, there is a school of thought that suggests that software generated for the Internet will grow in importance and eventually prevail in personal computing. If this were to happen, it would indirectly affect our business too. I'll examine this in more depth in Chapter 9.

"10X" Change: Regulation

Until now, we have followed the possible changes that can take place when one of the six forces affecting the competitive well-being of a business changes by a "10X" factor. That diagram illustrates the workings of a free market—unregulated by any external agency or government. But in real business life, such regulations—their appearance or disappearance—can bring about changes just as profound as any that we have discussed.

The demise of patent medicines

The history of the American drug industry provides a dramatic example of how the environment can change with the onset of regulation. At the start of the twentieth century, patent medicines made up of alcohol and narcotics were peddled freely without any labels to warn consumers of the dangerous and addictive nature of their contents. The uncontrolled proliferation of patent medicines finally triggered the government into the business of regulating what was put into the bottles, and led to the passage of a law requiring manufacturers of all medicines to label the ingredients of their elixirs. In 1906, the Food and Drugs Act was passed by Congress.

The drug industry changed overnight. The introduction of the labeling requirement exposed the fact that patent medicines were spiked with everything from alcohol to morphine to cannabis to cocaine, and forced their manufacturers to reformulate their products or take them off the shelves. The competitive landscape changed in the wake of the passage of the Food and Drugs Act. Now a company that wanted to be in the drug business needed to develop knowledge and skills that were substantially different from before. Some companies navigated through this strategic inflection point; many others disappeared.

The reordering of telecommunications

Regulatory changes have been instrumental in changing the nature of other very large industries. Consider the American telecommunications industry.

Prior to 1968, the U.S. telecommunications industry was practically a nationwide monopoly. AT&T—"the telephone company"—designed and manufactured its own equipment, ranging from telephone handsets to switching systems, and provided all connections between phone calls, both local and long distance. Then, in 1968, the Federal Communications Commission ruled that the phone company could not require the use of its own equipment at the customer's location.

This decision changed the landscape for telephone handsets and switching systems. It opened the business up to foreign equipment manufacturers, including the major Japanese telecommunications companies. The business that had been the domain of the slow-moving, well-oiled monopoly of the benign "Ma Bell" became rife with competition from the likes of Northern Telecom of Canada, NEC and Fujitsu from Japan, and Silicon Valley startups like ROLM. Telephone handsets, which the customer used to receive as part of the service from the old AT&T, now became commodities to be purchased at the corner electronics store. They were largely made at low labor cost in countries in Asia and they came in all sorts of shapes, sizes and functions, competing aggressively in price. And the familiar ringing of the telephone was supplanted by a cacophony of buzzes.

But all this was only a prelude to even bigger events.

In the early 1970s the U.S. Government, following a private antitrust suit by AT&T competitor MCI, brought suit, demanding the breakup of the Bell system and asking for the separation of long-distance services from local-access services. The story goes that after years of wrangling in the federal courts, a struggle which promised to go on for many more years, Charles Brown, then chairman of AT&T, one morning called his staff one at a time and told them that instead of putting the company through many years of litigation with an uncertain outcome, he would voluntarily go along with the breakup of the company. By 1984 this decision became the basis for what is known as the Modified Final Judgment, supervised by Federal Judge Harold Greene, that prescribed the way long-distance companies were to conduct business with the seven regional telephone companies. The telephone service monopoly crumbled, practically overnight.

I called on AT&T locations in those days to sell Intel microprocessors to their switching systems divisions. I still remember the profound state of bewilderment of AT&T managers. They had been in the same business for most of their professional lives and simply had no clue as to how things would go now that the customary financial, personal and social rules by which they had conducted themselves, division to division, manager to manager, were broken.

The impact of those events on the entire communications industry was equally dramatic. A competitive long-distance industry was created. Over the subsequent decade, AT&T lost 40 percent of the long-distance market to a number of competitors, some of whom, like MCI and Sprint, became multibillion-dollar companies themselves. A new set of independent companies operating regional telephone systems, often called the Baby Bells, were created. Each of these, with revenues in the $10 billion range, was left the task of connecting individuals and companies in their area to each other and to a competitive long-distance network. The Modified Final Judgment let them operate as monopolies in their own areas, subject to a variety of restrictions in terms of the businesses they might or might not participate in.

The Baby Bells themselves now face a similar upheaval, as changes in technology prompt further regulatory moves. The evolution of cellular telephony and a cable network that reaches 60 percent of U.S. houses provides alternative ways of connecting to the individual customers. Even as I write this, Congress labors to catch up with the impact of these changes in technology. No matter which way the telecommunications act will be rewritten, no matter how much the Charlie Chaplins and Seymour Crays of telephony fight the changes, they are coming. On the other side of this inflection point there will be a far more competitive business landscape for all aspects of the telecommunications business.

Of course, in retrospect it is easy to see that the creation of pharmaceutical regulations ninety years ago and the events that shaped the current telecommunications industry a decade ago clearly represented strategic inflection points for those industries. It is harder to decide whether the crosscurrents you are experiencing right now represent one.

Privatization

Much of the world is embroiled in what I want to call the "mother of all regulatory changes," privatization. Companies that have had a long history of operating as state-owned monopolies, from China to the former Soviet Union to the United Kingdom, at the stroke of a pen are being placed in a competitive environment. They have no experience of how to deal with competition. They never had to market to consumers; after all, why would a monopoly have to court customers?

AT&T, for example, had no experience dealing with competition, so they never had to market their products or services. They had all the customers that there were. Their management grew up in a regulatory environment where their core competencies revolved around their ability to work with the regulators; their work force was accustomed to a paternalistic work environment.

In the ten years of the free-for-all that followed the Modified Final Judgment, AT&T lost 40 percent of the long-distance market. However, they also mastered consumer marketing skills. Now AT&T advertises on television for new customers, makes a point of thanking you for using AT&T every time you connect with them and has even developed a distinctive sound to signal their presence—a sort of warm and fuzzy bong—all examples of world-class consumer marketing by a company where marketing used to be seen as a foreign art.

Deutsche Bundespost Telekom, Germany's state-owned telecommunications company, is slated to be liberalized by the end of

1997. To steer the renamed Deutsche Telekom through the troubled waters, the company's supervisory board recently appointed a forty-five-year-old consumer marketing manager from Sony to be its next CEO. This action suggests that the board understands that the future will be very, very different from the past.

When most companies of a previously regulated economy are suddenly thrust into a competitive environment, the changes multiply. Management now has to excel at marketing their services in the midst of a global cacophony of competing products, and every person on the labor force suddenly must compete for his or her job with employees of similar companies on the other side of the globe. This is the greatest strategic inflection point of all. When such fundamental changes hit a whole economy simultaneously, their impact is cataclysmic. They affect an entire country's political system, its social norms and its way of life. This is what we see in the former Soviet Union and, in a more controlled fashion, in China.

In this chapter I have tried to show that strategic inflection points are common; that they are not just a contemporary phenomenon, that they are not limited to the high-tech industry, nor are they something that only happens to the other guy. They are all different yet all share similar characteristics. The table on page 77 provides a snapshot of what the examples in this chapter illustrate. As I scan it, I can't help but be impressed by the variety and pervasiveness of strategic inflection points.

Note that everywhere there are winners and losers. And note also that, to a large extent, whether a company became a winner or a loser was related to its degree of adaptability. Strategic inflection points offer promises as well as threats. It is at such times of fundamental change that the cliché "adapt or die" takes on its true meaning.

Strategic Inflection Points:
Changes and Results

Example (category)	What changed	Action taken	Result
Wal-Mart (competition)	Superstores entered small communities	Some stores specialize, e.g., become category killers	Home Depot and Toys"Я"-Us thrive; many stores perish
Next (competition)	PCs with Windows took over	Next becomes a software company	Next survives as a small but profitable company
Talkies (technology)	Silent movies died	Greta Garbo speaks	Garbo becomes a star; other former stars fade
Shipping (technology)	New technology increased productivity	Singapore and Seattle adapt to container-ization; San Francisco and New York do not	Singapore and Seattle ports prosper; San Francisco and New York ports decline
PCs (technology)	PCs' price/performance was superior	Some companies adapt micro-computers as building blocks; others become systems integrators	Adaptive companies thrive; others face difficulties
Demographic time bomb (customers)	Kids have increased computer affinity	Growth of CD-ROM educational and entertainment software, aimed at kids	Computers become ubiquitous
Travel agencies (suppliers)	Airlines capped commissions	Travel agents charge consumers	Travel agency economics turn tougher
Telecommunications (regulation)	Competition in equipment and long-distance service	AT&T adapts to a competitive world with consumer marketing	AT&T and the Bell companies' combined valuation is over four times what it was ten years before
Privatization (regulations)	End of government monopolies and subsidies	Deutsche Telekom appoints Ron Sommer as CEO	Painful adjustments ahead

"Why Not Do It Ourselves?"

''The memory business crisis—and how we dealt with it—is how I learned the meaning of a strategic inflection point.''

Managing, especially managing through a crisis, is an extremely personal affair.

Many years ago, in a management class I attended, the instructor played a scene from the World War II movie *Twelve o'Clock High.* In this movie, a new commander is called in to straighten out an unruly squadron of fliers who had become undisciplined to the point of self-destruction. On his way to take charge, the new commander stops his car, steps out and smokes a cigarette, while gazing off into the distance. Then he draws one last puff, throws the cigarette down, grinds it out with his heel and turns to his driver and says, "Okay, Sergeant, let's go." Our instructor played this scene over and over to illustrate a superbly enacted instance of building up the determination necessary to undertake the hard, unpleasant and treacherous task of leading a group of people through an excruciatingly tough set of changes—the moment when a leader decides to go forward, no matter what.

I always related to this scene and empathized with that officer. Little did I know when I watched that movie that I would have to go through something similar in a few years' time. But beyond experiencing this crisis personally, the incident that I'm about to describe is how I learned with every fiber of my being what a strategic inflection point is about and what it takes to claw your way through one, inch by excruciating inch. It takes objectivity, the willingness to act on your convictions and the passion to mobilize people into supporting those convictions. This sounds like a tall order, and it is.

The story I'm going to tell you is about how Intel got out of the business it was founded on and how it refocused its efforts on and built a new identity in a totally different business—all in the midst of a crisis of mammoth proportions. I learned an enormous amount about managing through strategic inflection points as a result of this experience, and throughout the rest of this book, I will refer back to these events to illustrate what I learned. I'm afraid I have to drag you through some details. Bear with me. While the story is unique to Intel, the lessons, I believe, are universal.

Some history: Intel started in 1968. Every start-up has some kind of a core idea. Ours was simple. Semiconductor technology had grown capable of being able to put an ever larger number of transistors on a single silicon chip. We saw this as having some promising implications. An increasing transistor count readily translates into two enormous benefits for the customer: lower cost and higher performance. At the risk of some oversimplification, these come about as follows. Roughly speaking, it costs the same to produce a silicon chip with a larger number of transistors as a chip with a smaller number of transistors, so if we put more transistors on a chip, the cost per transistor would be lower. Not only that, smaller transistors are in closer proximity to each other and therefore handle electronic signals faster, which translates into higher performance in whatever finished gadget—calculator, VCR or computer—our chip should be placed into.

When we pondered the question of what we could do with this growing number of transistors, the answer seemed obvious: build chips that would perform the function of memory in computers. In other words, put more and more transistors on a chip and use them to increase the capacity of the computer's memory. This approach would inevitably be more cost-effective than any other method, we reasoned, and the world would be ours.

We started modestly. Our first product was a 64-bit memory. No, this is not a typo. It could store 64 digits—numbers. Today people are working on chips that can store 64 million digits but this is today and that was then.

It turns out that, around the time Intel started, one of the then major computer companies had called for proposals to build exactly such a device. Six companies, all established in the business, had already bid on the project. We muscled our way in as the seventh bidder. We worked day and night to design the chip and, in parallel, develop the manufacturing process. We worked as if our life depended on it, as in a way it did. From that project emerged the first functional 64-bit memory. As the first to produce a working chip, we won the race. This was a big win for a start-up!

Next we poured our efforts into developing another chip, a 256-bit memory. Again, we worked day and night, and this was an even harder job. Thanks to a great deal of effort, we introduced our second product a short while after the first.

These products were marvels of 1969 technology and it seemed that every engineer in every organization of every computer maker as well as every semiconductor maker bought one of each to marvel over. Very few people, however, bought production volumes of either. Semiconductor memories were not much more than curiosity items at that time. So we continued to burn cash and went on to develop the next chip.

In the tradition of the industry, this chip would contain more transistors than the previous chip. We aimed at a memory chip that was four times more complex, containing 1,024 digits. This required taking some big technological gambles. But we plugged on, memory engineers, technologists, test engineers and others, a hard-working, if not always harmonious, team. As a result of the pressure we felt, we often spent as much time bickering with one another as working on the problems. But work went on. And this time we hit the jackpot.

This device became a big hit. Our new challenge became how to satisfy demand for it. To put this in perspective, we were a company composed of a handful of people with a new type of design and a fragile technology, housed in a little rented building, and we were trying to supply the seemingly insatiable appetite of large computer companies for memory chips. The incredibly tough task of development segued into the nightmare of producing a device that was held together with the silicon equivalent of baling wire and chewing gum. The name of this device was the 1103. To this day, when a digital watch shows that number, I and other survivors of that era still take note.

Through our struggle with the first two technological curiosities that didn't sell and with the third one that sold but that we had such a hard time producing, Intel became a business and memory chips became an industry. As I think back, it's clear to me that struggling with this tough technology and the accompanying manufacturing problems left an indelible imprint on Intel's psyche. We became good at solving problems. We became highly focused on tangible results (our word for it is "output"). And from all the early bickering, we developed a style of ferociously arguing with one another while remaining friends (we call this "constructive confrontation").

As the first mover, we had practically 100 percent share of the memory chip market segment. Then, in the early seventies, other companies entered and they won some business. They were small American companies, similar to us in size and makeup. They had names like Unisem, Advanced Memory Systems and Mostek. If you don't recognize the names, it's because these companies are long gone.

By the end of the seventies there were maybe a dozen players in the business, each of us competing to beat the others with the latest technological innovations. With each succeeding generation of memory chips, somebody, not necessarily the same company, got it right and it certainly wasn't always us. A prominent financial analyst of the day used to report his observations of the memory business using boxing-match analogies: "Round Two goes to Intel, Round Three goes to Mostek, Round Four to Texas Instruments, we're gearing up to fight Round Five" . . . and so on. We won our share. Even ten years into this business, we were one of the key participants. Intel still stood for memories; conversely, memories meant (usually) Intel.

Entering Our Strategic Inflection Point

Then, in the early eighties, the Japanese memory producers appeared on the scene. Actually, they had first shown up in the late seventies to fill the product shortages we had created when during a recession we pulled back our investments in production capacity. The Japanese were helpful then. They took the pressure off us. But in the early eighties they appeared in force—in overwhelming force.

Things started to feel different now. People who came back from visits to Japan told scary stories. At one big Japanese company, for instance, it was said that memory development activities occupied a whole huge building. Each floor housed designers working on a different memory generation, all at the same time: On one floor were the 16K people (where "K" stands for 1,024 bits), on the floor above were the 64K people and on the floor above that people were working on 256K-bit memories. There were even rumors that in secret projects people were working on a million-bit memory. All this was very scary from the point of view of what we still thought of as a little company in Santa Clara, California.

Then we were hit by the quality issue. Managers from Hewlett-Packard reported that quality levels of Japanese memories were consistently and substantially better than those produced by the American companies. In fact, the quality levels attributed to Japanese memories were beyond what we thought were possible. Our first reaction was denial. This had to be wrong. As people often do in this kind of situation, we vigorously attacked the ominous data. Only when we confirmed for ourselves that the claims were roughly right did we start to go to work on the quality of our product. But we were clearly behind.

As if this weren't enough, the Japanese companies had capital advantages. They had (or were said to have) limitless access to funds—from the government? from the parent company through cross subsidies? or through the mysterious workings of the Japanese capital markets that provided nearly infinite low-cost capital to export-oriented producers? We didn't know exactly how it all worked but the facts were incontrovertible: As the eighties went on, the Japanese producers were building large and modern factories, amassing a capacity base that was awesome from our perspective.

Riding the memory wave, the Japanese producers were taking over the world semiconductor market in front of our eyes. This penetration into the world markets didn't happen overnight; as shown in the figure below, it took place over a decade.

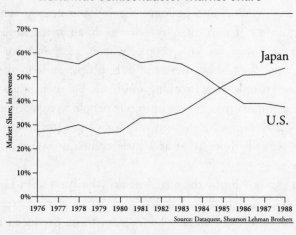

Worldwide Semiconductor Market Share

Source: Dataquest, Shearson Lehman Brothers

We fought hard. We improved our quality and brought costs down but the Japanese producers fought back. Their principal weapon was the availability of high-quality product priced astonishingly low. In one instance, we got hold of a memo sent to the sales force of a large Japanese company. The key portion of the memo said, "Win with the 10% rule. . . . Find AMD [another American company] and Intel sockets. . . . Quote 10% below their price . . . If they requote, go 10% AGAIN. . . . Don't quit till you WIN!"

This kind of thing was clearly discouraging but we fought on. We tried a lot of things. We tried to focus on a niche of the memory market segment, we tried to invent special-purpose memories called value-added designs, we introduced more advanced technologies and built memories with them. What we were desperately trying to do was to earn a premium for our product in the marketplace as we couldn't match the Japanese downward pricing spiral. There was a saying at Intel at that time: "If we do well we may get '2X' [twice] the price of Japanese memories, but what good does it do if 'X' gets smaller and smaller?"

Most importantly, we continued to spend heavily on R&D. After all, we were a company based on technology and we thought that every problem should have a technological solution. Our R&D was spread among three different technologies. Most of it was spent on memory chips. But at the same time a smaller team worked on technology for another device we had invented in 1970 or so: microprocessors. Microprocessors are the brains of the computer; they calculate while memory chips merely store. Microprocessors and memories are built with a similar silicon chip technology but microprocessors are designed differently than memories. And because they represented a slower-growing, smaller-volume market than memory chips, we didn't stress their technological development as heavily.

The bulk of the memory chip development took place in a

spanking new facility in Oregon. The microprocessor technology developers had to share a production facility—not even a new one at that—with the manufacturing folks at a remote site. Our priorities were formed by our identity; after all, memories *were* us.

While the situation on the memory front was tough, life was still good. In 1981, our then leading microprocessor was designed into the original IBM PC, and demand for it exploded far ahead of IBM's expectation. IBM, in turn, looked to us to help them ramp up production of the IBM PC. So did all of IBM's PC competitors. In 1983 and the early part of 1984 we had a heated-up market. Everything we made was in short supply. People were pleading with us for more parts and we were booking orders further and further out in time to guarantee a supply. We were scrambling to build more capacity, starting factory construction at different locations and hiring people to ramp up our production volumes.

Then in the fall of 1984 all of that changed. Business slowed down. It seemed that nobody wanted to buy chips anymore. Our order backlog evaporated like spring snow. After a period of disbelief, we started cutting back production. But after the long period of buildup, we couldn't wind down fast enough to match the market slide. We were still building inventory even as our business headed south.

We had been losing money on memories for quite some time while trying to compete with the Japanese producers' high-quality, low-priced, mass-produced parts. But because business had been so good, we just kept at it, looking for the magical answer that would give us a premium price. We persevered because we could afford to. However, once business slowed down across the board and our other products couldn't take up the slack, the losses really started to hurt. The need for a different memory strategy, one that would stop the hemorrhage, was growing urgent.

We had meetings and more meetings, bickering and arguments, resulting in nothing but conflicting proposals. There were those who proposed what they called a "go for it" strategy: "Let's build a gigantic factory dedicated to producing memories and nothing but memories, and let's take on the Japanese." Others proposed that we should get really clever and use an avant-garde technology, "go for it" but in a technological rather than a manufacturing sense and build something the Japanese producers couldn't build. Others were still clinging to the idea that we could come up with special-purpose memories, an increasingly unlikely possibility as memories became a uniform worldwide commodity. Meanwhile, as the debates raged, we just went on losing more and more money. It was a grim and frustrating year. During that time we worked hard without a clear notion of how things were ever going to get better. We had lost our bearings. We were wandering in the valley of death.

I remember a time in the middle of 1985, after this aimless wandering had been going on for almost a year. I was in my office with Intel's chairman and CEO, Gordon Moore, and we were discussing our quandary. Our mood was downbeat. I looked out the window at the Ferris wheel of the Great America amusement park revolving in the distance, then I turned back to Gordon and I asked, "If we got kicked out and the board brought in a new CEO, what do you think he would do?" Gordon answered without hesitation, "He would get us out of memories." I stared at him, numb, then said, "Why shouldn't you and I walk out the door, come back and do it ourselves?"

The Route to Survival

With that comment and with Gordon's encouragement, we started on a very difficult journey. To be completely honest about it, as I started to discuss the possibility of getting out of the memory chip business with some of my associates, I had a hard time getting the words out of my mouth without equivocation. It was just too difficult a thing to say. Intel equaled memories in all of our minds. How could we give up our identity? How could we exist as a company that was not in the memory business? It was close to being inconceivable. Saying it to Gordon was one thing; talking to other people and implementing it in earnest was another.

Not only was I too tentative as I started discussing this course of action with colleagues, I was also talking to people who didn't want to hear what I meant. As I got more and more frustrated that people didn't want to hear what I couldn't get myself to say, I grew more blunt and more specific in my language. The more blunt and specific I got, the more resistance, both overt and covert, I ran into.

So we debated endlessly. I remember at the end of a discussion asking one of our senior managers to write down what he understood our position to be on the subject; he was waffling as he struggled with the decision and I figured I could trap him with his own written memo. I failed. Months went by as we played these weird games.

In the course of one of my visits to a remote Intel location, I had dinner with the local senior managers, as I usually do. What they wanted to talk about was my attitude toward memories. I wasn't ready to announce that we were getting out of the business yet because we were still in the early stages of wrestling with the implications of what getting out would mean—among them, what work would we have for this very group of people afterward? Yet I couldn't get myself to pretend that nothing like this could ever happen. So I gave an ambivalent-to-negative answer, which this group immediately picked up on. One of them attacked me aggressively, asking, "Does it mean that you can conceive of Intel without being in the memory business?" I swallowed hard and said, "Yes, I guess I can." All hell broke loose.

The company had a couple of beliefs that were as strong as religious dogmas. Both of them had to do with the importance of memories as the backbone of our manufacturing and sales activities. One was that memories were our "technology drivers." What this phrase meant was that we always developed and refined our technologies on our memory products first because they were easier to test. Once the technology had been debugged on memories, we would apply it to microprocessors and other products. The other belief was the "full-product-line" dogma. According to this, our salesmen needed a full product line to do a good job in front of our customers; if they didn't have a full product line, the customer would prefer to do business with our competitors who did.

Given the strength of these two beliefs, an open-minded, rational discussion about getting out of memories was practically impossible. What were we going to use for technology drivers? How were our salespeople going to do their jobs when they had an incomplete product family?

So it was on that night at this Intel dinner I described above. The rest of the evening was spent going in circles around these two issues, the management group and I getting increasingly frustrated with each other.

This was typical of discussions on the subject. In fact, the senior manager in charge of our memory business couldn't get with the program even after months of discussions. Eventually he was offered a different job and accepted it, and I started with his replacement by spelling out exactly what I wanted him to do: *Get us out of memories!* By this time, having had months of frustrating discussions under my belt, I no longer had any difficulty making myself clear. Still, after the new person got acquainted with the situation, he took only half a step. He announced that we would do no further R&D on new products. However, he convinced me to finish what his group had in the works. In other words, he convinced me to continue to do R&D for a product that he and I both knew we had no plans to sell. I suppose that even though our minds were made up about where we were going our emotions were still holding both of us back from full commitment to the new direction.

I rationalized to myself that such a major change had to be accomplished in a number of smaller steps. But in a few months we came to the inevitable conclusion that this halfway decision was untenable and we finally worked up our determination and clearly decided—not just in the management ranks but throughout the whole organization—that we were getting out of the memory business, once and for all.

After all manner of gnashing of teeth, we told our sales force to notify our memory customers. This was one of the great bugaboos: How would our customers react? Would they stop doing business with us altogether now that we were letting them down? In fact, the reaction was, for all practical purposes, a big yawn. Our customers knew that we were not a very large factor in the market and they had half figured that we would get out; most of them had already made arrangements with other suppliers.

In fact, when we informed them of the decision, some of them reacted with the comment, "It sure took you a long time." People who have no emotional stake in a decision can see what needs to be done sooner.

I believe this has a great deal to do with why there is such a high turnover in the ranks of CEOs today. Every day, it seems, leaders who have been with the company for most of their working lives announce their departure, usually as the company is struggling through a period that has the looks of a strategic inflection point. More often than not, these CEOs are replaced by someone from the outside.

I suspect that the people coming in are probably no better managers or leaders than the people they are replacing. They have only one advantage, but it may be crucial: unlike the person who has devoted his entire life to the company and therefore has a history of deep involvement in the sequence of events that led to the present mess, the new managers come unencumbered by such emotional involvement and therefore are capable of applying an impersonal logic to the situation. They can see things much more objectively than their predecessors did.

If existing management want to keep their jobs when the basics of the business are undergoing profound change, they must adopt an outsider's intellectual objectivity. They must do what they need to do to get through the strategic inflection point unfettered by any emotional attachment to the past. That's what Gordon and I had to do when we figuratively went out the door, stomped out our cigarettes and returned to do the job.

As we came back in that door, the main question we faced was this: if we are not doing memories, what should our future focus be? Microprocessors were the obvious candidate. We had now been supplying the key microprocessors for IBM-compatible PCs for nearly five years; we were the largest factor in the market. Furthermore, our next mainline microprocessor, the "386," was ready to go into production. As I mentioned, its development was based on a technology developed in the corner of an old production plant. It would really have done much better in our most modern plant in Oregon but until now that place had been busy doing memory development. Getting out of the memory business gave us the opportunity to assign the group of developers in Oregon, who were arguably the best at Intel at this time, to the task of adapting their manufacturing process to build faster, cheaper, better 386s.

So I went up to Oregon. On the one hand, these developers were worried about their future. On the other hand, they were memory developers whose interest in and attachment to microprocessors was not very strong. I gathered them all in an auditorium and made a speech. The theme of the speech was, "Welcome to the mainstream." I said that Intel's mainstream was going to be microprocessors. By signing up to do microprocessor development, they would be bearing the flag for Intel's mainline business.

It actually went a lot better than I had expected. These people, like our customers, had known what was inevitable before we in senior management faced up to it. There was a measure of relief that they no longer had to work on something that the company wasn't fully committed to. This group, in fact, threw itself into microprocessor development and they have done a bang-up job ever since.

Elsewhere, however, the story was not so positive. These were very hard times and we were losing a lot of money. We had to lay off thousands of employees. We had no immediate use for the silicon fabrication plant where memories were made and had to shut it down. We also shut down assembly plants and testing plants that were involved with the production of memories. These also happened to be our oldest factories, situated in odd locations and too small for our business at this point anyway, so shutting them down gave us the opportunity to modernize our factory network. But that didn't make it any less painful.

Looking Back

It was through the memory business crisis—and how we dealt with it—that I learned the meaning of a strategic inflection point. It's a very personal experience. I learned how small and helpless you feel when facing a force that's "10X" larger than what you are accustomed to. I experienced the confusion that engulfs you when something fundamental changes in the business, and I felt the frustration that comes when the things that worked for you in the past no longer do any good. I learned how desperately you want to run from dealing with even describing a new reality to close associates. And I experienced the exhilaration that comes from a set-jawed commitment to a new direction, unsure as that may be. Painful as it has all been, it turned me into a better manager.

I learned some basic principles, too.

I learned that the word "point" in strategic inflection point is something of a misnomer. It's not a point; it's a long, torturous struggle.

In this case, the Japanese started beating us in the memory business in the early eighties. Intel's performance started to slump when the entire industry weakened in mid-1984. The conversation with Gordon Moore that I described occurred in mid-1985. It took until mid-1986 to implement our exit from memories. Then it took another year before we returned to profitability. Going through the whole strategic inflection point took us a total of three years. And while today, ten years later, they now seem compressed to one short and intense period, at the time, those three years were long and arduous—and wasteful. While we were fighting the inevitable, trying out all sorts of clever marketing approaches, looking for a niche that couldn't possibly exist in a commodity market, we were wasting time, getting deeper into red ink and ultimately forcing ourselves to take harsher actions to right things when we finally got around to taking action at all. While the realization of what we were facing was a flash of insight that took place in a single conversation, the work of implementing the consequences of that conversation went on for years.

I also learned that strategic inflection points, painful as they are for all participants, provide an opportunity to break out of a plateau and catapult to a higher level of achievement. Had we not changed our business strategy, we would have been relegated to an immensely tough economic existence and, for sure, a relatively insignificant role in our industry. By making a forceful move, things turned out far better for us.

What happened subsequently? The 386 became very, very successful, by far our most successful microprocessor to that point. Its success was greatly enhanced by the work of the former memory group in Oregon.

We were no longer a semiconductor memory company. As we started to search for a new identity for the corporation, we realized that all of our efforts now were devoted to the microprocessor business. We decided to characterize ourselves as a "microcomputer company." This started first in our public statements, literature and advertising but over the years, as the 386 became a phenomenal success, it took hold of the hearts and minds of our management and most of our employees. Eventually the outside world started to look at us that way too.

By 1992, mostly owing to our success with microprocessors, we became the largest semiconductor company in the world, larger even than the Japanese companies that had beaten us in memories. And by now our identification with microprocessors is so strong that it's difficult for us to get noticed for our nonmicroprocessor products.

Yet had we dithered longer, we could have missed our chance at all this. We might have vacillated between a heroic effort to hang on to our dwindling share of the memory business and an effort that might have been too weak to project us into the exploding microprocessor market. Had we stayed indecisive, we might have lost both.

One last lesson, and this is a key one: while Intel's business changed and management was looking for clever memory strategies and arguing among themselves, trying to figure out how to fight an unwinnable war, men and women lower in the organization, unbeknownst to us, got us ready to execute the strategic turn that saved our necks and gave us a great future.

Over time, more and more of our *production* resources were directed to the emerging microprocessor business, not as a result of any specific strategic direction by senior management but as a result of daily decisions by middle managers: the production planners and the finance people who sat around the table at endless production allocation meetings. Bit by bit, they allocated more and more of our silicon wafer production capacities to those lines which were more profitable, like microprocessors, by taking production capacity away from the money-losing memory business. Simply by doing their daily work, these middle managers were adjusting Intel's strategic posture. By the time we made the decision to exit the memory business, only one out of eight silicon fabrication plants was producing memories. The exit decision had less drastic consequences as a result of the actions of our middle managers.

This is not unusual. People in the trenches are usually in touch with impending changes early. Salespeople understand shifting customer demands before management does; financial analysts are the earliest to know when the fundamentals of a business change.

While management was kept from responding by beliefs that were shaped by our earlier successes, our production planners and financial analysts dealt with allocations and numbers in an objective world. For us senior managers, it took the crisis of an economic cycle and the sight of unrelenting red ink before we could summon up the gumption needed to execute a dramatic departure from our past.

Were we unusual? I don't think so. I think Intel was a well-managed company with a strong corporate culture, outstanding employees and a good track record. After all, we weren't quite seventeen years old, and in those seventeen years we had created several major business areas. We were good. But when we were caught up in a strategic inflection point, we almost missed it; we nearly became another Unisem, another Mostek, another Advanced Memory Systems.

"Signal" or "Noise"?

''How do we know
whether a change
signals a strategic
inflection point? The
only way is through
the process of
clarification that
comes from broad and
intensive debate.''

When is a change really a strategic inflection point? Changes take place in business all the time. Some are minor, some are major. Some are transitory, some represent the beginning of a new era. They all need to be dealt with but they don't all represent strategic inflection points.

How do you know what a certain set of changes represents? Put in another way, how can you tell the "signal" from the "noise"?

Is X-ray Technology a "10 X" Force?

Some years ago, key technologists at IBM told their counterparts at Intel and other companies that the Japanese semiconductor manufacturers were investing in gigantic and extremely expensive facilities for manufacturing semiconductors with even finer features than could be accomplished by ordinary techniques. These facilities would use x-rays instead of ordinary light to define the features of a chip. According to the IBM people, the Japanese had more than a dozen of these plants under construction. They feared that the Japanese investment in x-ray technology represented a fundamental change in the way semiconductors were built, a change by which the American producers could be left behind once and for all. If they were right, the x-ray approach would represent a "10X" technology factor and lead to an inflection point that we might never recover from.

IBM considered these developments a very major danger and decided to invest in x-ray equipment in a big way. Our people took this news very seriously. IBM technologists were extremely competent and their perception of the threat was ominous. Nor were they alone in this view. Nevertheless, after studying the issue, the Intel technologists decided that x-ray techniques were fraught with problems and that they were not production-worthy. Most importantly, they felt that our current technology could evolve to achieve ever finer features well into the future.

The way IBM and Intel responded to the x-ray technology threat showed that one company deemed it "signal," while the other classified it "noise." We decided not to pursue the x-ray approach. (Ten years later, it appears that we were right. As of this time of writing, to my knowledge, neither IBM nor the Japanese manufacturers are planning to use x-ray technology in manufacturing any time soon.)

In this case, competent and serious-minded people came to a different set of conclusions about a given set of facts. This is not at all uncommon. There simply is no surefire formula by which you can decide if something is signal or noise. But *because* there is no surefire formula, every decision you make should be carefully scrutinized and reexamined as time passes. Ten years ago, we decided that x-ray technology was not a "10X" factor. However, we continued to watch it, looking to see if the threat grew, waned or stayed the same.

Think of the change in your environment, technological or otherwise, as a blip on your radar screen. You can't tell what that blip represents at first but you keep watching radar scan after radar scan, looking to see if the object is approaching, what its speed is and what shape it takes as it comes closer. Even if it lingers on your periphery, you still keep an eye on it because its course and speed may change.

So it is with x-ray technology. It is on our radar screen and has been for years. Today, we still don't think we need to invest in it.

But a year from now, three years from now, five years from now, as we exhaust other means that are—for now—more cost-effective, the balance might shift and what we once correctly determined was noise might well emerge as a signal we had better pay heed to. These things are not cut and dried, and even if they were, things change. Therefore, you have to pay eternal attention to developments that could become a "10X" factor in your business.

RISC versus CISC

As potential "10X" factors go, the x-ray technology issue was relatively simple. Technologists at IBM had one opinion, their counterparts at Intel had another. We did what our collective judgment indicated we should do.

Things get a lot more complicated when the differences of opinion are not just between ourselves and others but when we argue inside the company as well. The story of the ferocious "RISC" versus "CISC" debates (which continue to this day) provide a good example of such a situation. RISC and CISC are acronyms for arcane computer terms—Reduced Instruction Set Computing and Complex Instruction Set Computing. For our purposes, it's enough to know that they describe two different ways of designing computers and, therefore, microprocessors.

The debate over their merits divided the computing industry and almost tore it apart. CISC was the older approach; RISC was a newer technique. CISC designs require a lot more transistors to achieve the same result that RISC chips can accomplish with fewer transistors.

Intel's chips are based on the older CISC scheme. By the time other companies started to pursue RISC techniques in the late eighties, the then current Intel microprocessor, the 386, was on the market, and the next generation Intel microprocessor, the 486, was in development. The 486 was a higher-performance, more advanced version of the same architecture that we used in the 386; it ran the same software but it ran it better. This was an extremely important consideration at Intel; we were (and are) determined that all our new microprocessors would be compatible with the software our customers bought for their earlier microprocessors.

Some of our people took the position that the RISC approach represented a "10X" improvement, a level of improvement that in the hands of others could threaten our core business. So, to hedge our bets, we put a big effort into developing a high-performance microprocessor based on RISC technology.

This project had a major drawback, however. Even though the new RISC chip was faster and cheaper, it would have been incompatible with most of the software that was available in the marketplace. Compatibility of a product was—and still is—a big factor in making it popular; therefore the idea that we would come up with an incompatible chip was not an appealing one. To get under the management radar screen that guarded our compatibility dogma, the engineers and technical managers who believed RISC would be a better approach camouflaged their efforts and advocated developing their chip as an auxiliary one that would work with the 486. All along, of course, they were hoping that the power of their technology would propel their chip into a far more central role. In any event, the project proceeded and eventually gave birth to a new and very powerful microprocessor, the i860.

We now had two very powerful chips that we were introducing at just about the same time: the 486, largely based on CISC technology and compatible with all the PC software, and the i860, based on RISC technology, which was very fast but compatible with nothing. We didn't know what to do. So we introduced both, figuring we'd let the marketplace decide.

However, things were not that simple. Supporting a microprocessor architecture with all the necessary computer-related products—software, sales and technical support—takes enormous resources. Even a company like Intel had to strain to do an adequate job with just one architecture. And now we had two different and competing efforts, each demanding more and more internal resources. Development projects have a tendency to want to grow like the proverbial mustard seed. The fight for resources and for marketing attention (for example, when meeting with the customer, which processor should we highlight?) led to internal debates that were fierce enough to tear apart our microprocessor organization. Meanwhile, our equivocation caused our customers to wonder what Intel really stood for, the 486 or the i860?

I was watching these developments with growing unease. The issue concerned the heart of our company, the microprocessor business that we had put our faith in and repositioned the company around when we abandoned the memory business just a few years earlier. It didn't involve factors that might or might not arise a decade from now, like x-ray technology; it demanded a decision immediately, and the decision was crucial. On the one hand, if the RISC trend represented a strategic inflection point and we didn't take appropriate action, our life as a microprocessor leader would be very short. On the other hand, the 386's fantastic momentum seemed sure to extend into the 486 and perhaps even to future generations of microprocessors. Should we abandon a good thing, which for now at least was a sure thing, and lower ourselves back down into a competitive battle with the other RISC architectures, a battle in which we had no particular advantage?

Although I have a technical background, it is not in computer science and I was not that comfortable with the architectural issues involved. To be sure, we had lots of people who had the right background but they had all split into warring camps, each camp 100 percent convinced of its own chip's supremacy.

Meanwhile, our customers and other industry partners were not of one mind either. On the one hand, the CEO of Compaq, a major and very technically savvy customer of ours, leaned on us—on me, in particular—and encouraged us to put all our efforts into improving the performance of our older CISC line of microprocessors. He was convinced that the architecture had enough power in it to last the rest of the decade, and he was unhappy seeing us split our resources and spend lots of time and money on something that was of no use to Compaq. On the other hand, the key technology manager at Microsoft, the company that provided most of the software that our customers used in conjunction with our microprocessors, was encouraging us to move toward an "860 PC." As the head of one of our European customers told me, "Andy, this is like the fashion business. We need something new."

When the 486 was formally introduced, the reaction of the customer community was extremely positive. I remember sitting at the product introduction in Chicago with a virtual Who's Who of the computer manufacturing world, all of whom showed up to announce their readiness to build 486-based computers, and thinking, "RISC or no RISC, how could we possibly not put all our efforts into supporting this momentum?" After this event, the debates were over and we refocused our efforts on the 486 and its successors.

Looking back at these debates six years after the fact, I shake my head about how I could have even considered walking away from our traditional technology that then had, and still has, phenomenal headroom and momentum. Today, in fact, the advantages of RISC technology over CISC technology are much smaller than they appeared then. Yet at that time we were seriously considering a major shift of resources.

Is It or Isn't It?

Sometimes the event that signals a strategic inflection point is dramatically clear. I doubt that it required a lot of study to conclude that the Modified Final Judgment that led to the breakup of the old AT&T was a monumental event. It probably was also pretty clear that when the FDA was formed and the truth-in-labeling act was passed, the world of patent medicine changed once and for all. There was no question that these events represented key changes in the environment of the businesses that operated under their influence.

Most of the time it's not like that. Most strategic inflection points, instead of coming in with a bang, approach on little cat feet. They are often not clear until you can look at the events in retrospect. Later, when you ask yourself when you first had an inkling that you were facing a strategic inflection point, your recollections are about a trivial sign hinting that the competitive dynamics had changed. In the earlier story about memories, Intel visitors to Japan came back with the report that Japanese businessmen who had previously been very respectful of us now seemed to look at us with a newfound derision. "Something changed, it's different now," people said when they returned from Japan. And this comment and observations like it heightened our awareness that a real change was upon us.

So how do you know whether a change signals a strategic inflection point?

Ask these questions to attempt to distinguish signal from noise:

- Is your key competitor about to change? First, figure out who your key competitor is by asking a hypothetical question that I call the "silver bullet" test. It works like this: if you had just one bullet in a figurative pistol, whom among your many competitors would you save it for? Asked point-blank, this question usually provokes a visceral response and I find that people can normally give an answer without much hesitation. When the answer to this question stops being as crystal clear as it used to be and some of your people direct the silver bullet to competitors who didn't merit this kind of attention previously, it's time to sit up and pay special attention. When the importance of your competitors shifts, it is often a sign that something significant is going on.

- In an analogous fashion, you should ask, is your key complementor about to change? Does the company that in past years mattered the most to you and your business seem less important today? Does it look like another company is about to eclipse them? If so, it may be a sign of shifting industry dynamics.

- Do people seem to be "losing it" around you? Does it seem that people who for years had been very competent have suddenly gotten decoupled from what really matters? Think about it. You and your management have both been selected by the evolutionary forces of your business to be at the top of your organization. Your genes were right for the original business. But if key aspects of the business shift around you, the very process of genetic selection that got you and your associates where you are might retard your ability to recognize the new trends. A sign of this might be that all of a sudden some people "don't seem to get it." Conversely, it may be that you yourself are often inclined to shake your head in confusion. When they don't get it or you don't get it, it may not be because of encroaching age; it may be because the "it" has changed around you.

Helpful Cassandras

The Cassandras in your organization are a consistently helpful element in recognizing strategic inflection points. As you might remember, Cassandra was the priestess who foretold the fall of Troy. Likewise, there are people who are quick to recognize impending change and cry out an early warning.

Although they can come from anywhere in the company, Cassandras are usually in middle management; often they work in the sales organization. They usually know more about upcoming change than the senior management because they spend so much time "outdoors" where the winds of the real world blow in their faces. In other words, their genes have not been selected to achieve perfection in the old way.

Because they are on the front lines of the company, the Cassandras also feel more vulnerable to danger than do senior managers in their more or less bolstered corporate headquarters. Bad news has a much more immediate impact on them personally. Lost sales affect a salesperson's commission, technology that never makes it to the marketplace disrupts an engineer's career. Therefore, they take the warning signs more seriously.

The other night, I checked my electronic mailbox and found a message from our sales manager in charge of the Asia-Pacific region. He passed on some breaking news from his area that had to do with a potential competitive element. His story was a familiar enough scenario—and yet as he began to talk about the new item, his tone was quite concerned, almost scared. "I don't mean to be an alarmist and I know that situations like this come up all the time but this one really concerns me . . . ," he wrote. He was in no position to suggest a course of action; he was just asking me to pay attention to this development and urging me to take it seriously.

My immediate reaction was to shrug off his news. I feel much safer back here in California than he does in "enemy territory." But is my perspective the right one? Or is his? After all, being there doesn't automatically make him right in his assessment. I could claim to have a better overall perspective on things. Yet I have learned to respect changes in the tone of messages from people in the field. I will watch further developments of this news item more carefully than I would have otherwise and, in fact, I have since decided to initiate a broader study of its potential implications.

You don't have to seek these Cassandras out; if you are in management, they will find you. Like somebody who sells a product that he is passionate about, they will "sell" their concern to you with a passion. Don't argue with them; even though it's time-consuming, do your best to hear them out, to learn what they know and to understand why it affects them the way it does.

Classify the time you spend listening to them as an investment in learning what goes on at the distant periphery of your business, whether you think of distances in geographical or technological terms. Think of it this way: when spring comes, snow melts first at the periphery, because that's where it's most exposed. Factoring in the news from the periphery is an important contribution to the process of sorting out signal from noise.

There is a fine distinction here. When I say, "Learn what goes on at the periphery of your business," it means something different than if I had said, "Learn what goes on in your business." In the ordinary course of business, I talk with the general manager, with the sales manager, with the manufacturing manager. I learn from them what goes on in the business. But they will give me a perspective from a position that is not terribly far from my own. When I absorb news or information coming from people who are geographically distant or who are several levels below me in the organization, I will triangulate on business issues with their view, which comes from a completely different perspective. This will bring insights that I would not likely get from my ordinary contacts.

Of course, you can't spend all of your time listening to random inputs. But you should be open to them. As you keep doing it, you will develop a feel for whose views are apt to contain gems of information and a sense of who will take advantage of your openness to clutter you with noise. Over time, then, you can adjust your receptivity accordingly.

Sometimes a Cassandra brings not tidings of a disaster but a new way of looking at things. During the height of Intel's RISC versus CISC debate, when I was most confused, our chief technologist asked to see me. He sat down and methodically took me through his point of view while at the same time representing the other side's argument in the most objective way that I heard. His knowledge and insights made up for my own lack of self-confidence and expertise in this area and helped me listen to the ongoing debates with a better grasp of what I was hearing. Although this encounter did not lead me to a firm position, it helped me form a framework in which to better evaluate everyone else's arguments.

In the case of Intel's exit from the memory business, how did Intel, the memory company, get to where only one factory out of eight was producing memory chips by the mid-1980s, making our exit from memories less cataclysmic? It got there by the autonomous actions of the finance and production planning people, who sat around painstakingly allocating wafer production capacity month by month, moving silicon wafers from products where they seemed wasteful—memories were the prime example of this—to other products which seemed to generate better margins, such as microprocessors. These people didn't have the authority to get us out of memories but they had the authority to fine-tune the production allocation process by lots of little steps. Over the course of many months, their actions made it easier to eventually pull the plug on our memory participation.

Peter Drucker quotes a definition of an entrepreneur as someone who moves resources from areas of lower productivity and yield to areas of higher productivity and yield. That's what a properly motivated and intelligent middle manager will do with resources under his or her command. The resources can range from wafer allocation for a production planner to how a salesperson schedules his or her efforts and energy. Are these random actions on the part of middle management or are they strategy being formed and executed? To be sure, they don't seem strategic at first glance but I think they are.

Avoiding the Trap of the First Version

Helpful Cassandras are quick to notice the first signs of "10X" forces but those signs are often mixed in with symptoms of forces that might appear to be "10X" but aren't. For instance, is the Internet really that big a deal? Are we going to do all our banking electronically? Is interactive television going to transform our lives? Are digital media going to transform the entertainment industry?

The first thing you should realize is that everybody with a gadget hawks and hypes it and consciously or unconsciously works double time to make their product as important as possible. Under the circumstances, it's only natural to be suspicious and so you should be.

The second thing is that, when you explore these developments first hand, you'll discover that mostly they aren't what they're cracked up to be. In the early days, getting from one place to another on the Internet took forever and when you got there, more often than not, you found a stale marketing brochure. Electronic banking is still a clumsy way to replace a stamp. And interactive television seems to have vanished even before the ink dried on the mega-announcements.

On the other hand, don't shut off your radar screens and go on about your business, discounting everything even if at first it seems quite crummy. A danger in assessing the significance of changes lies in what I call the trap of the first version.

In 1984, when Apple introduced the Macintosh, I thought it was a ridiculous toy. Among other weaknesses I saw in it, it didn't have a hard disk (at the time, all PCs already had one) and it was excruciatingly slow. Because of these two factors, the Mac's graphical interface struck me as more of a nuisance than a significant advantage. The first implementation of the Mac blinded me to the far more important features that came with graphical interfaces, like the fact that they brought with them a uniformity for all the application programs that were based on them: You learned one and you learned them all. But I didn't see through the problems of the first version to perceive the beauty of the technology that lay beneath them.

In 1991, when Apple started to talk about the hand-held computing devices called personal digital assistants, or PDAs, a lot of people both inside and outside Intel considered them a "10X" force capable of restructuring the PC industry. PDAs could do to PCs what PCs were doing to mainframes, many said. Not wanting to be blind to this possibility, we made a very substantial external investment and started a major internal effort to ensure that we would participate in any PDA wave in a big way. Then Apple's Newton came out in 1993 and was promptly criticized for its failings.

What does this say about the PDA phenomenon? Is it less of a "10X" force because its first instantiation was disappointing? When you think about it, first versions of most things usually are. Lisa, the first commercial computer with a graphical user interface and the predecessor of the Mac, did not receive good acceptance. Neither did the first version of Windows, which was considered an inferior product for years—DOS with a pretty face, as many called it. Yet graphical user interfaces in general, and Windows in particular, have become "10X" forces shaping the industry.

My point is that you can't judge the significance of strategic inflection points by the quality of the first version. You need to draw on your experience. Perhaps you remember your reaction to the first PC you ever saw. It probably didn't strike you as a revolutionary device. So it is with the Internet. Now, as you stare at your computer screen that's connected to the Internet, waiting for a World Wide Web page to slowly materialize, let your imagination flow a bit. What might this experience be like if transmission speed doubled? Or better yet, if it were improved by "10X"?

What might the content look like if professional editors rather than amateurs created it, not as a sideline but as their main occupation? You might extrapolate the evolution of this phenomenon by remembering how rapidly PCs evolved and improved.

As you consider this or any new device, your answer may be that, even if it were "10X" better, it wouldn't interest you as a consumer. Even if a company actually supplied it, it wouldn't change the silver bullet test and it wouldn't rearrange your complementors. Life would go on as before, just with one more gadget.

But if your instincts suggest that a "10X" improvement could make this capability exciting or threatening, you may very well be looking at the beginning of what is going to be a strategic inflection point. Consequently, you must discipline yourself to think things through and separate the quality of the early versions from the longer-term potential and significance of a new product or technology.

Debate

The most important tool in identifying a particular development as a strategic inflection point is a broad and intensive debate. This debate should involve technical discussions (for example, is RISC inherently "10X" faster?), marketing discussions (is it a fashion fling or is it a business?) and considerations of strategic repercussions (how will it affect our microprocessor business if we make a dramatic move; how will it affect it if we don't?).

The more complex the issues are, the more levels of management should be involved because people from different levels of management bring completely different points of view and expertise to the table, as well as different genetic makeups.

The debate should involve people outside the company, customers and partners who not only have different areas of expertise but also have different interests. They bring their own biases and their own interests into the picture (as Compaq's CEO did when he urged us to continue with CISC development) but that's okay: a business can succeed only if it serves the interests of outside parties as well.

This kind of debate is daunting because it takes a lot of time and a lot of intellectual ergs. It also takes a lot of guts; it takes courage to enter into a debate you may lose, in which weaknesses in your knowledge may be exposed and in which you may draw the disapproval of your coworkers for taking an unpopular viewpoint. Nevertheless, this comes with the territory and when it comes to identifying a strategic inflection point, unfortunately, there are no shortcuts.

If you are in senior management, don't feel you're being a wimp for taking the time to solicit the views, convictions and passions of the experts. No statues will be carved for corporate leaders who charge off on the wrong side of a complex decision. Take your time until the news you hear starts to repeat what you've already heard, and until a conviction builds up in your own gut.

If you are in middle management, don't be a wimp. Don't sit on the sidelines waiting for the senior people to make a decision so that later on you can criticize them over a beer—"My God, how could they be so dumb?" Your time for participating is now. You owe it to the company and you owe it to yourself. Don't justify holding back by saying that you don't know the answers; at times like this, nobody does. Give your most considered opinion and give it clearly and forcefully; your criterion for involvement should be that you're heard and understood. Clearly, all sides cannot prevail in the debate but all opinions have value in shaping the right answer.

What if you are not in management at all? What if you are a salesperson, a computer architect or a technologist who manages no one? Should you leave the decisions to others? On the contrary, your firsthand knowledge eminently qualifies you as a know-how manager. As a potentially full-fledged participant in these debates, what you may miss in perspective and breadth you make up in the depth of your hands-on experience.

It is important to realize what the purpose of these debates is and what it isn't. Don't think for a moment that at the end of such debates all participants will arrive at a unanimous point of view. That's naive. However, through the process of presenting their own opinions, the participants will refine their own arguments and facts so that they are in much clearer focus. Gradually all parties can cut through the murkiness that surrounds their arguments, clearly understand the issues and *each other's* point of view. Debates are like the process through which a photographer sharpens the contrast when developing a print. The clearer images that result permit management to make a more informed—and more likely correct—call.

The point is, strategic inflection points are rarely clear. Well-informed and well-intentioned people will look at the same picture and assign dramatically different interpretations to it. So it is extraordinarily important to bring the intellectual power of all relevant parties to this sharpening process.

If the prospect of a vigorous debate scares you, it's understandable. Lots of aspects of managing an organization through a strategic inflection point petrify the participants, senior management included. But inaction might lead to a bad result for your business and that should frighten you more than anything else.

Arguing with the Data

Contemporary management doctrine suggests that you should approach any debate and argument with data in hand. It's good advice. Altogether too often, people substitute opinions for facts and emotions for analysis.

But data are about the past, and strategic inflection points are about the future. By the time the data showed that the Japanese memory producers were becoming a major factor, we were in the midst of a fight for our survival.

At the risk of sounding frivolous, you have to know when to hold your data and when to fold 'em. You have to know when to argue with data. Yet you have to be able to argue *with* the data when your experience and judgment suggest the emergence of a force that may be too small to show up in the analysis but has the potential to grow so big as to change the rules your business operates by. The point is, when dealing with emerging trends, you may very well have to go against rational extrapolation of data and rely instead on anecdotal observations and your instincts.

Fear

Constructively debating tough issues and getting somewhere is only possible when people can speak their minds without fear of punishment.

The quality guru W. Edwards Deming advocated stamping out fear in corporations. I have trouble with the simplemindedness of this dictum. The most important role of managers is to create an environment in which people are passionately dedicated to winning in the marketplace. Fear plays a major role in creating and maintaining such passion. Fear of competition, fear of bankruptcy, fear of being wrong and fear of losing can all be powerful motivators.

How do we cultivate fear of losing in our employees? We can only do that if we feel it ourselves. If we fear that someday, any day, some development somewhere in our environment will change the rules of the game, our associates will sense and share that dread. They will be on the lookout. They will be constantly scanning their radar screens. This may bring a lot of spurious warnings of strategic inflection points that turn out to be false alarms, but it's better to pay attention to these, to analyze them one at a time and make an effort to dispose of them, than to miss the significance of an environmental change that could damage your business forever.

It is fear that makes me scan my e-mail at the end of a long day, searching for problems: news of disgruntled customers, potential slippages in the development of a new product, rumors of unhappiness on the part of key employees. It is fear that every evening makes me read the trade press reports on competitors' new developments and leads me to tear out particularly ominous articles to take to work for follow-up the next day. It is fear that gives me the will to listen to Cassandras when all I want to do is cry out, "Enough already, the sky *isn't* falling," and go home.

Simply put, fear can be the opposite of complacency. Complacency often afflicts precisely those who have been the most successful. It is often found in companies that have honed the sort of skills that are perfect for their environment. But when their environment changes, these companies may be the slowest to respond properly. A good dose of fear of losing may help sharpen their survival instincts.

That's why in a way I think that we at Intel were fortunate to have gone through the terrible times in 1985 and 1986 that I described in Chapter 5. Most of our managers still remember what it felt like to be on the losing side. Those memories make it easy to conjure up the lingering dread of a decline and generate the passion to stay out of it. It may sound strange but I'm convinced that the fear of repeating 1985 and 1986 has been an important ingredient in our success.

But if you are a middle manager you face an additional fear: the fear that when you bring bad tidings you will be punished, the fear that your management will not want to hear the bad news from the periphery. Fear that might keep you from voicing your real thoughts is poison. Almost nothing could be more detrimental to the well-being of the company.

If you are a senior manager, keep in mind that the key role of Cassandras is to call your attention to strategic inflection points, so under no circumstances should you ever "shoot the messenger," nor should you allow any manager who works for you to do so.

I can't stress this issue strongly enough. It takes many years of consistent conduct to eliminate fear of punishment as an inhibitor of strategic discussion. It takes only one incident to introduce it. News of this incident will spread through the organization like wildfire and shut everyone up.

Once an environment of fear takes over, it will lead to paralysis throughout the organization and cut off the flow of bad news from the periphery. An expert in market research once told me how at her company every layer of management between her and the chief executive watered down her fact-based research. "I don't think they want to hear that" was the byword with which bad news was eliminated, bit by bit, data point by data point, as her information was advanced along the management chain. Senior management in this company didn't have a chance. Bad news never reached them. This company has gone from greatness to real tough times. Watching them from the outside, it seemed that management didn't have a clue as to what was happening to them. I firmly believe that their tradition of dealing with bad news was an integral part of their decline.

I have described how our Asia-Pacific sales manager and a key technologist came to see me with their warnings and/or perceptions. Both of them were long-term employees, self-confident and comfortable with Intel's culture. They were results-oriented and familiar with constructive confrontation; they understood how these help us collectively to make better decisions and come to better solutions. They knew how we go about doing things and how we don't—rules that you don't find written down anywhere. Both overcame their hesitation and took what might be seen as a risk. One came to tell me a piece of news that he felt was a serious problem; it might have been a valid warning or he might have thought he was foolish to raise it but he knew he could mention his misgivings without fear of repercussion. The other could explain his views on RISC designs with the unstated premise of, "Hey, Grove, you're out of your depth here, let me teach you a few things."

From our inception on, we at Intel have worked very hard to break down the walls between those who possess knowledge power and those who possess organization power. The salesperson who knows his territory, the computer architect and engineer who are steeped in the latest technology possess knowledge power. The people who marshal or shuffle resources, set budgets, assign staff and remove them from projects possess organizational power. One is not better than the other in managing strategic change. Both of them need to give their best to guide the corporation to good strategic results. Ideally, each will respect the other for what he or she brings to the party and will not be intimidated by the other's knowledge or position.

An environment like this is easy to describe but hard to create and maintain. Dramatic or symbolic moves do nothing. It requires living this culture, promoting constant collaborative exchanges between the holders of knowledge power and the holders of organizational power to create the best solutions in the interest of both. It requires rewarding those who take risks when pursuing their jobs. It requires making adherence to the values by which we operate part of the formal management performance process. And, as a last recourse, it requires parting ways with those who can't find it in themselves to adapt. I think whatever success we have had in maintaining our culture has been instrumental in Intel's success in surviving strategic inflection points.

Let Chaos Reign

''Resolution comes through experimentation. Only stepping out of the old ruts will bring new insights.''

With all the rhetoric about how management is about change, the fact is that we managers loathe change, especially when it involves us. Getting through a strategic inflection point involves confusion, uncertainty and disorder, both on a personal level if you are in management and on a strategic level for the enterprise as a whole. These two levels are more intimately connected than one might think.

The Touchy-Feely Issues

How a company handles the process of getting through a strategic inflection point depends predominantly on a very "soft," almost touchy-feely issue: how management reacts emotionally to the crisis.

This is not so strange. Businesspeople are not just managers; they are also human. They have emotions, and a lot of their emotions are tied up in the identity and well-being of their business.

If you are a senior manager, you probably got to where you are because you have devoted a large portion of your life to your trade, to your industry and to your company. In many instances, your personal identity is inseparable from your lifework. So, when your business gets into serious difficulties, in spite of the best attempts of business schools and management training courses to make you a rational analyzer of data, objective analysis will take second seat to personal and emotional reactions almost every time.

If you are a middle manager, many of the same considerations apply. But very often your job is also at stake. How your corporation succeeds in working its way through a strategic inflection point may determine what happens to your career.

A manager in a business that's undergoing a strategic inflection point is likely to experience a variation of the well-known stages of what individuals go through when dealing with a serious loss. This is not surprising, because the early stages of a strategic inflection point are fraught with loss—loss of your company's preeminence in the industry, of its identity, of a sense of control of your company's destiny, of job security and, perhaps the most wrenching, the loss of being affiliated with a winner. However, unlike the accepted model of the sequence of emotions associated with grief (i.e., denial, anger, bargaining, depression and, ultimately, acceptance), in the case of a strategic inflection point, the sequence goes more as follows: denial, escape or diversion and, finally, acceptance and pertinent action.

Denial is prevalent in the early stages of almost every example of a strategic inflection point I can think of. During Intel's memory situation, I remember thinking, "If we had just started our development of the 16K memory chip earlier, the Japanese wouldn't have made any headway."

Escape, or diversion, refers to the personal actions of the senior manager. When companies are facing major changes in their core business, they seem to plunge into what seem to be totally unrelated acquisitions and mergers. In my view, a lot of these activities are motivated by the need of senior management to occupy themselves respectably with something that clearly and legitimately requires their attention day in and day out, something that they can justify spending their time on and make progress in instead of figuring out how to cope with an impending strategically destructive force.

At such times, senior managers often involve themselves in feverish charitable fundraising, a lot of outside board activities or pet projects. Take a look at a representative calendar of the CEO of a major corporation that was in the middle of a strategic inflection point (page 126). Does his allocation of time, his most precious resource, reflect the strategic crisis? I don't think so.

He is by no means unique. Frankly, as I look back, I have to wonder if it was an accident that I devoted a significant amount of my time in the years preceding our memory episode, years during which the storm clouds were already very evident, to writing a book. And as I write this, I wonder what storm clouds I might be ducking now. I'll probably know in a few years.

But let's go back to acquisitions, my favorite example. If I undertake a multibillion-dollar acquisition, every decision associated with it will require my attention. I will have to work so very hard and very quickly that the acquisition will take on far more importance than anything else that I have to deal with in the ordinary line of my business. So I will have created an infinite sink for my attention. I can justify looking in the mirror every morning and saying, "I don't have time to deal with such mundane issues as why we are gradually losing sales at the smaller accounts. I've got a very important midnight meeting with my investment advisers coming up." Under the circumstances, my inattention to daily details is understandable, even respectable; the acquisition has taken on a life of its own that takes me away from something that I don't know how to handle. I wonder to what extent all the acquisitions of movie studios by the major Japanese consumer electronics companies were motivated by the need of senior management to engage in diversions from the far more intractable and mundane problems of a secular slowdown of their core businesses.

These stages aren't just the province of bad senior managers.

Calendar of the CEO of a Major U.S. Corporation During a Strategic Inflection Point

MONDAY

8:30–9:30	Strategic planning conference update
10:00–10:30	Review plans for annual design award
11:00–12:00	Management and measurement systems
1:00–1:15	Review education speech
1:30–2:00	Quality update
4:00–4:45	Preparation for board meeting
5:25	Depart for East Coast city
6:30–9:30	Dinner meeting–outside board of directors
	Overnight in East Coast city

TUESDAY

8:00–9:00	Breakfast meeting
9:30	Depart for second East Coast city
11:00–11:45	Business association-education meeting
12:00–2:00	Business association–education task force
2:00–8:30	Business association board meeting
	Overnight in second East Coast city

WEDNESDAY

8:15–11:45	Charity executive committee
12:15–1:30	Travel to company headquarters
2:00–5:00	Executive staff meetings
6:00	Depart for East Coast factory
	Overnight in factory town

THURSDAY

3:30–5:00	Plant celebration, night shift
5:30–9:15	Second plant celebration
9:30–10:30	Third plant celebration
11:00–11:50	Fourth plant celebration
12:00	Depart for company headquarters
2:00–4:15	Executive Staff meetings

FRIDAY

8:15–8:30	Board meeting agenda
8:30–9:00	3rd quarter outlook
9:00–12:00	Executive staff meetings
1:15–5:00	Company review—U.S. division

Good leaders are also subject to the same emotional wriggling. They, however, eventually emerge to the acceptance and action phases. Lesser leaders are not capable of that and they are often removed. Then they are replaced by individuals who are not necessarily more capable but who do not have the emotional investment in the previous strategy.

This is a key point. The replacement of corporate heads is far more motivated by the need to bring in someone who is not invested in the past than to get somebody who is a better manager or a better leader in other ways.

The Inertia of Success

Senior managers got to where they are by having been good at what they do. And over time they have learned to lead with their strengths. So it's not surprising that they will keep implementing the same strategic and tactical moves that worked for them during the course of their careers—especially during their "championship season."

I call this phenomenon the inertia of success. It is extremely dangerous and it can reinforce denial.

When the environment changes in such a way as to render the old skills and strengths less relevant, we almost instinctively cling to our past. We refuse to acknowledge changes around us, almost like a child who doesn't like what he's seeing so he closes his eyes and counts to 100 and figures that what bothered him will go away. We too close our eyes and are willing to work harder, to dedicate ourselves to our traditional tasks or skills, in the hope that they and hard work will get us there by the count of 100. The phrase you're likely to hear at such times is "Just give us a bit more time."

Strategic Dissonance

As we begin to respond, maybe too little too late, we face another emotional hurdle: to admit to ourselves consciously and explicitly the magnitude of the problem we are struggling with. Even as our actions begin to reflect the process of adjusting to the new environment, we still struggle with the task of describing them in clear words. Recall the story of how Intel exited the memory business. The company had been adjusting wafer allocation for some time, yet when I was asked point-blank about our plans I had difficulty explaining them in plain English.

I have seen many companies fall into the same trap of saying one thing and doing another while they are in the midst of coping with a strategic inflection point. I call this divergence between actions and statements strategic dissonance. It is one of the surest indications that a company is struggling with a strategic inflection point.

Why is strategic dissonance so inevitable? What brings it about? The process of adapting to change starts with employees who, through their daily work, adjust to the new outside forces. The Intel production schedulers shifted wafer capacity from memories to microprocessors because the latter were more profitable. Meanwhile, we senior managers were trapped by the inertia of our previous success. After all, we had grown up as a memory producer: that's what we had been good at and that's what shaped our view of ourselves. Consequently, while front-line employees and middle managers were implementing and executing strategic actions that said one thing, senior management was still issuing high-level strategic pronouncements that said the exact opposite.

What tips you off to emerging strategic dissonance?

Signs of strategic dissonance often surface when senior managers engage their middle management or their sales force in a free-flowing discussion, provided that the discussion takes place in a culture that permits open confrontation. This is how it works at Intel. Occasionally, when I stand in front of such a group and field questions, I find it awkward to attempt to defend the position of the corporation in the face of some specific questions and comments that come from people who are wise to their world and their environment. Often these questions come in the form of follow-up questions after I have been asked about our specific strategy regarding a particular product, customer or technology. After I have given my well-practiced answer, the follow-up question may start with "But what about . . ." or "Does it mean that . . ."

Such questions usually represent sharp probing for the true intent behind the general answer I've just given. To be sure, they may be triggered by my not having been clear enough. But, on the other hand, they might be caused by a growing dissonance between my well-worn answer and a diverging reality. If it's the latter case, this may be the first sign of a strategic dissonance and prompts me to say to myself, "Grove, listen up, something is not quite right here."

Strategic dissonance is so much an automatic reaction to a strategic inflection point that probing for it is perhaps the best test of one. When people in the company start asking questions like "But how can we say 'X' when we do 'Y'?" more than anything else this is a tip-off that a strategic inflection point may very well be in the making.

Experimentation

While this dissonance between what the company does and what management says is understandable, it accompanies a terribly unproductive and distressing phase. The growing discomfort associated with strategic dissonance creates confusion and uncertainty even in the best of minds. You know that something substantial is not right—something is different—but you don't know what it is, you don't know how significant it really is and you don't know what to do about it.

Resolution of strategic dissonance does not come in the form of a figurative light bulb going on. It comes through experimentation. Loosen up the level of control that your organization normally is accustomed to. Let people try different techniques, review different products, exploit different sales channels and go after different customers. Much as management has been devoted to making and keeping order in the company, at times like this they must become more tolerant of the new and the different. Only stepping out of the old ruts will bring new insights.

The operating phrase should be: "Let chaos reign!"

Not that chaos is good in general. It's awfully inefficient and wearing on all participants. But the old order won't give way to the new without a phase of experimentation and chaos in between.

The dilemma is that you can't suddenly start experimenting when you realize you're in trouble unless you've been experimenting all along. It's too late to do it once things have changed in your core business. Ideally, you should have experimented with new products, technologies, channels, promotions and new customers all along. Then, when you sense that "something has changed," you will have a number of experiments that can be relied on to expand your bag of tricks and your organization will be in a much better position to expand the scope of experimentation and to tolerate the increased level of chaos that is the precursor for repositioning the company in a new business direction.

Intel experimented with microprocessors for over ten years before the opportunity and imperative arose to make them the centerpiece of our corporate strategy. During this period of time, microprocessors were not our main line; in fact, for a number of years we spent more money on developing and marketing them than they generated in revenue. But we kept at it, our microprocessor business gradually grew and, when our circumstances changed in a big way, we had a more appealing business to focus our resources on.

Experiments are not without controversy. Consider the conflict at Intel in the late 1980s between the i860 RISC processor and the 486 CISC processor described in Chapter 6. While our stated strategy was to be fully dedicated to maintaining a compatible family of microprocessors, we allowed some of our best people to put their efforts and creative energies into developing a new architecture in the form of the i860.

That was not all bad. Had the old technology run out of steam, embracing the new technology might very well have been the right thing for us to do. Experimenting with it gave us a head start to make such a shift, had it been necessary.

However, by letting this experiment grow and bubble up and reach the marketplace, the experiment itself grew to be a very large force affecting the company; it divided our efforts, muddied the waters about which microprocessor technology the company stood for and eventually could have weakened our entire microprocessor thrust. In short, it created chaos. We needed to deal with it one way or another, either by taking advantage of our momentum in the standard microprocessor market to create a new RISC branch, or by decisively reining in the experiment.

The Business Bubble

As in many sports, timing is everything. The same action taken in business early on may do the job; taken later on, it may well fall short because it won't be enough.

By "early" I mean acting while the momentum of your existing business is strong, while the cash flow is there and while the organization is intact. The momentum of a still healthy business provides you with a benign bubble within which you can work on repositioning the company. Under the protection of this bubble you can make changes far more easily than when the vital signs of your business have all turned south.

In other words, it is best when senior management recognizes and accepts the inevitability of a strategic inflection point early on and acts before the vitality of the business has been sapped by the "10X" forces affecting it. The necessary transformation of the business will likely be a lot less wrenching and more successful if proper action is taken early and enforced decisively.

The reality, unfortunately, is that we tend to do exactly the opposite. Owing precisely to the emotional factors described earlier, most management will do too little too late and therefore fritter away the protection that the bubble of their existing business would otherwise have provided them with.

It's easy to see why. There's no panic in the early stages of an inflection point. One can couch the arguments for inaction in the early stages in statements like "We shouldn't tinker with the golden goose" or "How could we possibly take our best people away from the business that pays all of our salaries and put them on some speculative new project?" or the most alarming one of all, "The organization can take just so much change; it's not ready for more," meaning really, *"I'm* not ready to lead the organization into the changes that it needs to face."

Looking back over my own career, I have never made a tough change, whether it involved resource shifts or personnel moves, that I haven't wished I had made a year or so earlier. Recall Intel's memory episode. We had been losing money in memories for quite some time. Yet we only reacted when the rest of our business went into a recession also. Next only acted when their cash needs forced them to. The previously immensely successful Compaq was slow to act forcefully as the personal computer business turned into a lower-margin, commodity-like business. It took a six-month decline in revenue, profits and market share, including a $70 million loss and its first-ever layoffs before Compaq's board of directors took draconian steps.

This tendency is easy to see in others although we are prone to blindness when we do it ourselves. The other day I met with a manager of a company that is struggling with a strategic change. I was urging him to act aggressively in adopting a new direction. It was easy for me to encourage him: After all, *I* didn't have to do anything, while *he* had to force his organization into a set of actions that would mean discontinuing some products that they had already committed to their customers. He knew that he needed to act; in fact, he *was* making some moves in the right direction. Yet these moves were pitifully inadequate in my view. They adjusted things at the margins—they dropped a few less successful versions of the product—whereas what he needed to do was discontinue the product altogether and redeploy development resources into obvious and far more promising directions. I wasn't any smarter than he; I was just unfettered by the responsibility of actually having to order up the changes. When, during Intel's memory crisis, I was in this manager's shoes, for a long time I too was guilty of the same too-little-too-late syndrome.

Ideally, the fear of a new environment sneaking up on us should keep us on our toes. Our sense of urgency should be aided by our judgment, instincts and observations that have been honed by decades spent in the business world. The fact is, because of our experience, very often we managers know that we need to do something. We even know what we should be doing. But we don't trust our instincts or don't act on them early enough to take advantage of the benign business bubble. We must discipline ourselves to overcome our tendency to do too little too late.

A New Industry Map

The too-little-too-late syndrome is particularly hazardous in a shifting industry environment. Implicit in doing business every day is a mental map of the structure of the industry. This map is composed of an unstated set of rules and relationships, ways and means of doing business, what's "done" and how it is done and what's "not done," who matters and who doesn't, whose opinion you can count on and whose opinion is usually wrong, and so on. If you've been in the industry for a long time, knowing these things has become second nature. You don't even think about them; you just know that's the way things are.

But when the structure of the industry changes, all of these elements change too. The mental map that you have been carrying with you all these years and relied upon in charting your company's course of action suddenly loses its validity. However, you haven't had a chance to replace it with a new mental map. You haven't made the explicit substitutions about how things are done now versus how they were done before, or who matters now versus who mattered then.

All of us in the computing industry had to deal with the concept of a transition from the vertical to the horizontal industry model. The fundamental implication of this model was—and is—that the player with the largest share of a horizontal layer is the one who wins. As this realization sank in at Intel, it reinforced our belief in the significance of compatibility with all of the rest of the horizontal layers and provided further encouragement for our drive toward high volume and low cost in our microprocessor business: toward improving our scale and scope. Likewise, when Compaq executed a major restructuring and strategic change in 1991, their actions also represented a recognition of the importance of scale and scope implicit in the horizontal model.

During a strategic inflection point, management continually has to refine its conception of the strategic map of the industry. We all automatically do this in our heads. But mental maps are awfully forgiving of ambiguity. You must force yourself to commit your thoughts to paper.

Where do you begin? Every company has organizational charts, sometimes piles of them, that show the interrelationship of the organizational units. If those are needed to help employees figure out how to operate inside a company, wouldn't an equivalent diagram of an industry be extremely helpful? So develop one. (In Chapter 9, I'll show an example of one that helped me to sort out some things about the Internet.)

Much as your business needs to experiment with new technologies and methods of distribution, as a senior manager, you need to experiment with filling in the details of the new industry structure. Try out your evolving map on your close associates. You will need to discuss it in a friendly audience many times to clarify your own mind. But there is another benefit, too: These discussions will help get your organization ready for change.

In a modern organization, rapid response to market forces depends on the autonomous actions of middle managers. Their ranks include know-how managers, the technical and marketing experts whose command of the fundamentals of the business is vital to the company's doing the right thing. If senior managers and know-how managers share a common view of the industry, the likelihood of their acknowledging changes in the environment and responding in an appropriate fashion will greatly increase. Sharing a common picture of the map of the industry and its dynamics is a key tool in making your organization an adaptive one.

Whether you are a senior manager, middle manager or know-how manager, as you improve your map, it will increasingly guide you toward better actions in your business and toward greater confidence that your actions are right.

Rein in Chaos

''Clarity of direction, which includes describing what we are going after as well as describing what we will *not* be going after, is exceedingly important at the late stage of a strategic transformation.''

When I think about what it's
like to get through a strategic inflection point, I'm reminded of a
classic scene in old western movies in which a bedraggled group of
riders is traveling through a hostile landscape. They don't know
exactly where they are going; they only know that they can't turn
back and must trust that they will eventually reach a place where
things are better.

Taking an organization through a strategic inflection point is a
march through unknown territory. The rules of business are unfamiliar or have not yet been formed. Consequently, you and your
associates lack a mental map of the new environment, and even
the shape of your desired goal is not completely clear.

Things are tense. Often in the course of traversing a strategic
inflection point your people lose confidence in you and in each
other, and what's worse, you lose confidence in yourself. Members
of management are likely to blame one another for the tough
times the company is experiencing. Infighting ensues, arguments
as to what direction to take bubble up and proliferate.

Then, at some point, you, the leader, begin to sense a vague
outline of the new direction. By this time, however, your company is dispirited, demoralized or just plain tired. Getting this far
took a lot of energy from you; you must now reach into whatever
reservoir of energy you have left to motivate yourself and, most
importantly, the people who depend on you so you can become
healthy again.

I think of this hostile landscape through which you and your company must struggle—or else perish—as the valley of death. It is an inevitable part of every strategic inflection point. You can't avoid it, nor can you make it less perilous, but you can do a better job of dealing with it.

Traversing the Valley of Death

To make it through the valley of death successfully, your first task is to form a mental image of what the company should look like when you get to the other side. This image not only needs to be clear enough for you to visualize but it also has to be crisp enough so you can communicate it simply to your tired, demoralized and confused staff. Will Intel be a broad-based semiconductor company, a memory company or a microprocessor company? Will Next be a computer company or a software company? What exactly is your bookstore going to be about—will it be a pleasant place to drink coffee and read or a place where you go to buy books at a discount?

You need to answer these questions in a single phrase that everybody can remember and, over time, can understand to mean exactly what you intended. In 1986, when we came up with the slogan "Intel, the microcomputer company," that was exactly what we were trying to achieve. The phrase didn't say anything about semiconductors, it didn't say anything about memories. It was meant to project our mental image of the company as we would emerge from the valley of death that the 1985–86 memory debacle/strategic inflection point represented for us.

Management writers use the word "vision" for this. That's too lofty for my taste. What you're trying to do is capture the essence of the company and the focus of its business. You are trying to define what the company will be, yet that can only be done if you also undertake to define what the company will *not* be.

Doing this should actually be a little easier at this point because, as you're coming out of a very bad period, you're likely to have extremely strong feelings about what you don't want to be. By 1986 we knew we did not want to be in the memory business any longer. We knew it with a passion that only comes after struggling with a business and finding that we were no better off for those struggles.

There are dangers in this approach: the danger of oversimplifying the identity of the company, of narrowing its strategic focus too much, so that some people will say, "But what about *my* part of the business . . . does this mean that we are no longer interested in that?" After all, Intel continued to do things other than microprocessors. We even continued to maintain a substantial business in a different type of semiconductor memories.

But the danger of oversimplification pales in comparison with the danger of catering to the desire of every manager to be included in the simple description of the refocused business, therefore making that description so lofty and so inclusive as to be meaningless.

Consider the following example that shows the value of a strong strategic focus. Lotus's identity for its first ten years was as a supplier of personal computer software, specifically spreadsheets. Owing to some missteps of their own but, most importantly, because of a "10X" increase in the forces of competition (what the Japanese memory producers were to us, Microsoft's presence in applications software was to them), Lotus's core business weakened over time. But while this was happening, Lotus had developed a new generation of software, embodied in their product Notes, that promised to bring the same kind of productivity gains to groups that spreadsheets had brought to individuals. Even as Lotus was struggling with spreadsheets and its related software business, its management committed itself to group computing to the extent of deemphasizing their spreadsheet business. It continued to invest in developing Notes throughout these difficult years and it mounted a major marketing and development program that suffused all the corporate statements.

To be sure, the story is still evolving. But from the standpoint of giving the company an unequivocal future, Lotus's management did exactly the right thing. It was Lotus's strength in Notes that ultimately motivated IBM to purchase the company for $3.5 billion.

Now consider an opposite example—of a company floundering to define itself. Recently, I met with a senior manager of a company with whom we were trying to collaborate to ensure that their product and our product worked together. To make this deal click, they needed to make some clear decisions about which technologies they were devoted to and which they weren't. I was dealing with a man at the second-highest level of his company, yet I found him torn and indecisive. On the one hand, he seemed convinced that we should work together; on the other hand, he seemed almost paralyzed when he needed to commit to the necessary actions to make this collaboration happen.

A couple of days later his boss, the chief executive officer, was quoted making statements about the company's intentions that unequivocally supported the direction I thought my visitor was leaning toward. I tore the article out of the newspaper, waved it in the face of my associates and announced, "I think we are in business." My euphoria lasted twenty-four hours. The next day's newspaper brought a retraction, described as a "clarification." It was all a big misunderstanding.

Now think for a moment of what it must be like to be a marketing or sales manager being buffeted by such ambiguities coming from your boss. Not only that, imagine what it would feel like to read about his direction *du jour* when it appears in the newspaper. How can you motivate yourself to continue to follow a leader when he appears to be going around in circles?

I can't help but wonder why leaders are so often hesitant to lead. I guess it takes a lot of conviction and trusting your gut to get ahead of your peers, your staff and your employees while they are still squabbling about which path to take, and set an unhesitating, unequivocal course whose rightness or wrongness will not be known for years. Such a decision really tests the mettle of the leader. By contrast, it doesn't take much self-confidence to downsize a company—after all, how can you go wrong by shuttering factories and laying people off if the benefits of such actions are going to show up in tomorrow's bottom line and will be applauded by the financial community?

Getting through strategic inflection points represents a fundamental transformation of your company from what you were to what you will be. The reason such a transformation is so hard is that all parts of the company were shaped by what you had been in the past. If you and your staff got your experience managing a computer company, how can you even imagine managing a software company? If you got your experience managing a broadbased semiconductor company, how can you even imagine what a microcomputer company might be like? Not surprisingly, the transformation implicit in surviving a strategic inflection point involves changing members of management one way or another.

I remember a meeting of our executive staff in which we were discussing Intel's new direction as a "microcomputer company." Our chairman, Gordon Moore, said, "You know, if we're really serious about this, half of our executive staff had better become software types in five years' time." The implication was that either the people in the room needed to change their areas of knowledge and expertise or the people themselves needed to be changed. I remember looking around the room, wondering who might remain and who might not. As it turned out, Gordon Moore was right. In our case, about half the management transformed themselves and were able to move in the new direction. Others ended up leaving the company.

Seeing, imagining and sensing the new shape of things is the first step. Be clear in this but be realistic also. Don't compromise and don't kid yourself. If you are describing a purpose that deep down you know you can't achieve, you are dooming your chances of climbing out of the valley of death.

Redeploying Resources

As Drucker suggests, the key activity that's required in the course of transforming an organization is a wholesale shifting of resources from what was appropriate for the old idea of the business to what is appropriate for the new. Over the three years that the production planners at Intel gradually cut the allotment of wafer production for memories and moved it to microprocessors, they were shifting rare and valuable resources from an area of lower value to an area of higher value. But raw materials are not your only resource.

Your best people—their knowledge, skills and expertise—are an equally important resource. When we recently assigned a key manager from overseeing our next generation of microprocessors to a brand-new communications product line which is not likely to make us money for several years, we were shifting an extremely valuable resource. While he was very productive in his former area, there were others equally good to take his place there, while the new area badly needed the turbocharging his presence would give it.

A person's time is an extremely valuable yet manifestly finite resource. When Intel was making its transformation from a "semiconductor company" to a "microcomputer company," I realized that I needed to learn more about the software world. After all, how we would do our job depended on the plans, thoughts, desires and visions of the software industry. So I deliberately started to spend a significant amount of time getting acquainted with software people. I set out to visit heads of software companies. I called them up one at a time, made appointments, met with them and asked them to talk to me about their business—as it were, to teach me.

This entailed some personal risk. It required swallowing my pride and admitting how little I knew about their business. I had to walk into conversations with important people whom I had never met, not having a clue how they would respond. It also required a measure of diligence; as I sat talking with these people, I took copious notes, some of which I understood and some of which I didn't. I then took the stuff that I didn't understand back to our internal experts and asked them to explain what this individual might have meant by it. Basically, I went back to school. (I was aided by the fact that Intel is a schoolish company, where it's perfectly respectable for a senior person with twenty years of experience to take some time, buckle down and learn a whole new set of skills.)

Admitting that you need to learn something new is always difficult. It is even harder if you are a senior manager who is accustomed to the automatic deference which people accord you owing to your position. But if you don't fight it, that very deference may become a wall that isolates you from learning new things. It all takes self-discipline.

The discipline of redeployment is needed in spades when it comes to your personal time. When I started on this software study, I had to take the time I spent on it away from other things. In other words, I had to be the "production planner" of my own time and had to reallocate the way I spent time at work. This brought with it its own difficulties because people who were accustomed to seeing me periodically no longer saw me as often as they used to. They started asking questions like, "Does this mean you no longer care about what we do?" I placated them as best I could, I reassigned tasks among other managers and, after a while, people accepted this as well as many other changes as being part of Intel's new direction. But it wasn't easy for them or me.

The point is that redeploying resources sounds like such an innocuous term: it implies that you're putting more attention and energy into something, which is wonderful, positive and encouraging. But the inevitable counterpart is that you're subtracting from someplace else. You're taking something away: production resources, managerial resources or your own time. A strategic transformation requires discipline and redeployment of all resources; without them, it turns out to be nothing more than an empty cliché.

One more word about your own time: if you're in a leadership position, how you spend your time has enormous symbolic value. It will communicate what's important or what isn't far more powerfully than all the speeches you can give.

Strategic change doesn't just start at the top. It starts with your calendar.

Leading Via Strategic Actions

Assigning or reassigning resources in order to pursue a strategic goal is an example of what I call strategic action. I'm convinced that corporate strategy is formulated by a series of such actions, far more so than through conventional top-down strategic planning. In my experience, the latter always turns into sterile statements, rarely gaining traction in the real work of the corporation. Strategic actions, on the other hand, always have real impact.

What's the difference? Strategic *plans* are statements of what we intend to do. Strategic *actions* are steps we have already taken or are taking which suggest our longer-term intent. Strategic *plans* sound like a political speech. Strategic *actions* are concrete steps. They vary: They can be the assignment of an up-and-coming player to a new area of responsibility; they can be the opening of sales offices in a portion of the world where we haven't done business before; they can be a cutback in the development effort that deals with a long-pursued area of our business. All of these are real and suggest directional changes.

While strategic *plans* are abstract and are usually couched in language that has no concrete meaning except to the company's management, strategic *actions* matter because they immediately affect people's lives. They change people's work, as was the case when we shifted capacity from memory production to microprocessor production and our sales force had a different product mix. They cause consternation and raise eyebrows, as did the transfer of the Intel manager from the tried-and-true microprocessor business to an ambiguous new area.

Strategic *plans* deal with events that are so far in the future that they have little relevance to what you actually have to do today. So they don't command true attention.

Strategic *actions,* however, take place in the present. Consequently, they command immediate attention. Their power comes from this very aspect. Even if any one strategic action changes the trajectory on which the corporation moves by only a few degrees, if those actions are consistent with the image of what the company should look like when it gets to the other side of the inflection point, every one of them will reinforce every other. That's why I think the most effective way to transform a company is through a series of incremental changes that are consistent with a clearly articulated end result.

Yet strategic inflection points are times that can also benefit from more drastic and higher-profile strategic actions. By higher profile, I mean that they are seen, heard and questioned by many people. Take the example I described earlier when the statement by the chief executive of the company we were trying to do business with was quoted in the newspaper. It caused a large number of raised eyebrows and scores of "Does this mean that . . . ?" questions. It afforded a perfect opportunity to reinforce a new strategic direction on a broad scale. Unfortunately, the next day's retraction laid waste to this opportunity.

But while it is good for strategic actions during an inflection point to raise eyebrows, they must also be timed just right. Strategic actions, especially those involving redeployment, are like the actions of runners in a relay race. Runners need to pass the baton at precisely the right moment; being even a little bit early or a little bit late will slow down the team.

The timing of the transfer of resources from the old to the new has to be done with this crucial balance in mind. If you move resources from the old business, the old task, the old product too early, you may leave a task only 80 percent finished. With a little bit more effort, you could have reaped the full benefit. On the other hand, if you hang on to the old business too long, the opportunity for grabbing a new business opportunity, to add momentum to a new product area, to get aligned with the new order of things, may be lost. There is a period in between that provides the best compromise, when you have invested enough in the old business that it has momentum to get you through the period of transition while you deploy your resources to the new target area. This timing dilemma is illustrated below.

Resource Shift Dilemma

RESOURCE SHIFT IS PREMATURE:	TIMING IS RIGHT:	RESOURCE SHIFT IS LATE:
previous task is not completed	momentum of existing strategy is still positive; new threat or opportunity has been verified	opportunity for transformation is lost; decline may be irreversible

When is the time right? When the momentum of your existing strategy is still positive, your business is still growing, your customers and complementors still think highly of you yet there's enough evidence of blips on your radar screen to warrant, at a minimum, exploring their significance. If your exploration confirms that they are real and are gaining, shift more resources on to them.

Your tendency will almost always be to wait too long. Yet the consequences of being early are less onerous than the consequences of being late. If you act too early, chances are the momentum of your previous business is still healthy. Therefore even if you're wrong, you're in a better position to course-correct. For instance, you can even pull back to their old jobs people whom you've reassigned to other areas. Since they come from those tasks, they can pick up the pieces again in no time and help out. But management's tendency is to hang on to the old, so their strategic actions are more likely to happen later rather than earlier. The risk is that if you are late you may already be in an irreversible decline.

Simply put, in times of change, managers almost always know which direction they should go in, but usually act too late and do too little. Correct for this tendency: Advance the pace of your actions and increase their magnitude. You'll find that you're more likely to be close to right.

The best moment to act varies from company to company. Some companies recognize that their key strengths are rapid response and fast execution. Such companies may profitably wait for others to test the limits of technological possibilities or market acceptance and then commit to following, catching up and passing them.

I describe such a strategy as a "taillight" approach. When you drive in the fog, it is a lot easier to drive fast if you're chasing the taillights of the car ahead of you. The danger with a "taillight" strategy is that, once you catch up and pass, you will find yourself without a set of taillights to follow—and without the confidence and competence in setting your own course in a new direction.

Being an early mover involves different risks. The biggest danger facing an early-mover company is that it may have a hard time distinguishing a signal from a noise and start to respond to an inflection point that isn't one. Moreover, even if it is right in its response, it is likely to be ahead of its market and will run a greater risk of getting caught up in the dangers of the "first instantiation," as described in Chapter 6.

But offsetting these dangers is the possibility of greater rewards: The early movers are the only companies that have the potential to affect the structure of the industry and to define how the game is played by others. Only by such a strategy can you hope to compete for the future and shape your destiny to your advantage.

In recent years, we at Intel decided that we have a tremendous opportunity to exploit the personal computer as a universal information appliance. This wasn't always possible; the traditional PC was largely used as a replacement for data entry terminals capable of displaying numbers and text appropriate only for commercial transactions. However, over the last several years, technology has brought appealing visual capabilities to the PC, endowing it with colorful graphics, sound and video, while retaining its important traditional characteristic: interactivity.

But while we saw the possibility of exploiting these capabilities and envisioned the PC as being in the middle of the information and entertainment revolution that was taking place around us, much of the rest of the world thought that all of these developments would take place around the more familiar television set. So we threw ourselves completely behind the concept that the PC would be the center of all these developments (the battle cry was "The PC Is It!") and launched an industry-wide campaign to proselytize our view. At the same time, we aligned all of our technical developments inside the company to make the PC an even more compelling choice for this task. We were—and still are—trying to shape our future at a time when this idea doesn't have broad currency. We were—and are—trying to be early movers.

A question that often comes up at times of strategic transformation is, should you pursue a highly focused approach, betting everything on one strategic goal, or should you hedge? The question may come in the form of an employee asking me, "Andy, shouldn't we be investing in areas other than microprocessors instead of putting all of our eggs in one basket?" or "Andy, shouldn't we work on enhancing the television set in addition to betting on personal computers?" I tend to believe Mark Twain hit it on the head when he said, "Put all of your eggs in one basket and WATCH THAT BASKET."

It takes every erg of energy in your organization to do a good job pursuing one strategic aim, especially in the face of aggressive and competent competition.

There are several reasons for this. First, it is very hard to lead an organization out of the valley of death without a clear and simple strategic direction. After all, getting there sapped the energy of your organization; it demoralized your employees and often set them against one another. Demoralized organizations are unlikely to be able to deal with multiple objectives in their actions. It will be hard enough to lead them out with a single one.

If competition is chasing you (and they always are—this is why "only the paranoid survive"), you only get out of the valley of death by outrunning the people who are after you. And you can only outrun them if you commit yourself to a particular direction and go as fast as you can. You could argue that, since they are chasing you, you should give yourself all sorts of alternative directions—in other words, hedge. I say, "No." Hedging is expensive and dilutes commitment. Without exquisite focus, the resources and energy of the organization will be spread a mile wide—and they will be an inch deep.

Second, while you're going through the valley of death, you

may think you see the other side, but you can't be sure whether it's truly the other side or just a mirage. Yet you have to commit yourself to a certain course and a certain pace, otherwise you will run out of water and energy before long.

If you're wrong, you will die. But most companies don't die because they are wrong; most die because they don't commit themselves. They fritter away their momentum and their valuable resources while attempting to make a decision. The greatest danger is in standing still.

The Clarity Imperative

When a company is meandering, its management staff is demoralized. When the management staff is demoralized, nothing works: Every employee feels paralyzed. This is exactly when you need to have a strong leader setting a direction. And it doesn't even have to be the best direction—just a strong, clear one.

Organizations in the valley of death have a natural tendency to drift back into the morass of confusion. They are very sensitive to obscure or ambiguous signals from their management.

Heads of companies often inadvertently contribute to this confusion. Some time ago a business reporter told me of an encounter with the head of a major Japanese corporation. The reporter was working on a profile of the company. When he asked questions that tried to clarify the strategy of the corporation, the other man angrily retorted, "Why would I tell you our strategy? So I could help our competitors?" I think this man wouldn't talk about his strategy not because he was afraid of helping his competitors but because he didn't have one: this company's public statements have always struck me as extraordinarily ambiguous.

Another way to fuel confusion is to give conflicting messages. At times of transition, pronouncements from the heads of organizations are painstakingly scrutinized and greatly amplified, especially by employees. Earlier I described an executive who retracted a statement about his company's strategic direction that had already appeared in the newspapers. After that retraction, his credibility had to have been damaged. He will have to work that much harder to impart direction and have people believe it. In other words, screw up once and it will take a lot more work later to communicate the right message to correct your mistake.

The point is this: how can you hope to mobilize a large team of employees to pull together, accept new and different job assignments, work in an uncertain environment and work hard despite the uncertainty of their future, if the leader of the company can't or won't articulate the shape of the other side of the valley?

Clarity of direction, which includes describing what we are going after as well as describing what we will *not* be going after, is exceedingly important at the late stage of a strategic transformation. Much as in the middle of the strategic inflection process you needed to let chaos reign in order to explore your alternatives, to lead your organization out of the resulting ambiguity and to energize your staff toward a new direction, you must rein in chaos.

The time for listening to the Cassandras is over. The time for experimentation is also over. The time to issue marching orders—exquisitely clear marching orders—to the organization is here. And the time to commit the resources of the corporation as well as your own resources—your own time, visibility, speeches, statements in external forums (which are always given more credibility inside the company than what you say directly to your employees)—is upon you. Most of all, you must be a role model of the new strategy. That is the best way to prove that you are committed to it.

How do you role-model a strategy? By showing your interest in the elements that lead to the strategic direction, by getting involved in the details that are appropriate to the new direction and by withdrawing attention, energy and involvement from those things that don't fit. Overcorrect your actions, recognizing that the symbolic nature of your actions will amplify their impact within the organization.

You can overcorrect by neglecting or overdelegating details in areas that, while still important, do not fit your immediate strategic needs. There's a danger in deemphasizing some important things but that's a risk you have to take. If, as a result of your overcorrection and neglect, some of the nuts and bolts of your daily work get dropped, you can always go back and pick them up later. What you can't correct is failing to make the appropriate high-profile strategic shift at the right moment.

At times like this, your calendar becomes your most important strategic tool. Most executives' schedules are shaped by the inertia of prior actions. You are likely to accept appointments, attend meetings and schedule activities that are similar to what you had been doing in the past. Break the mold now. Resist the tacit temptation to accept invitations or make appointments because you have done so in the past. Ask yourself the questions, "Will going to this meeting teach me about the new technology or the new market that I think is very important now? Will it introduce me to people who can help me in the new direction? Will it send a message about the importance of the new direction?" If so, go to it. If not, resist it.

The point is this: you can't hedge in a choice of direction and you can't hedge in your commitment to it. If you do, your people will be confused and after a while they will throw up their hands in resignation. Not only will you lose direction, but you will continue to sap the energy of your organization as well.

A difficulty in role-modeling a new strategic action is that leaders of large organizations, by the nature of their jobs, are often distanced from direct contact with many managers and employees. You can't talk to everybody; you can't look all of them in the eye and argue your point. So you need to find a way to project your determination, will and vision over a distance, much as the forces of a strong magnet affect iron filings.

When you have to reach large numbers of people, you can't possibly overcommunicate and overclarify. Give a lot of speeches to your employees, go to their workplaces, get them together and explain over and over what you're trying to achieve. (Take particular care to answer questions of the "Does it mean that . . ." variety. Those are the ones that offer the best chance of bringing your message home.) Your new thoughts and new arguments will take awhile to sink in. But you will find that repetition sharpens your articulation of the new direction and makes it increasingly clear to your employees. So speak and answer questions as often as possible; while it may seem like you're repeating yourself, in reality you will be reinforcing a strategic message.

Middle management has a special role to play here. More than anyone, middle management can help you project your message over a distance. By including them in your thinking and doing a particularly good job of enlisting them as sources of amplification of your new direction, you can multiply your presence many times. Take extra time with them because otherwise you risk losing their wholehearted commitment.

The best aspect of this type of exposure is that you will test whether you can pass the gauntlet of your employees' questions, assuming you have the kind of corporate culture in which they feel comfortable questioning you. Your employees' questions are usually shrewd, and in a free environment they can question you in a way that no one else can. If there is strategic illogic in your thinking, they will sniff it out and poke at it.

This is not fun. You may want to hide from exposing the holes in your strategic thinking—after all, having them on display in front of a group of your own employees would be embarrassing, wouldn't it? Yet I think it would be far better to let your employees find them when there's still time to make corrections than to allow the marketplace to find them later.

Technology can help you here. E-mail gives us a very powerful new way to reach large numbers of people. In most modern organizations, every computer is connected to a corporate network through which it can send messages to every other computer on that network. By spending minutes in front of his computer, a manager can leave his mark on the thoughts of dozens, hundreds or even thousands of people in his organization and do so with the immediacy that only the bounce of electronic communications can generate.

One caveat: if your message is clear, it will provoke questions and responses which will come back to you through the same medium. Answer them. You don't have to make a lot of time for that; a response of two or three lines can communicate the essence of your position. This is a high-leverage activity; your message will reach not just the individual to whom you are sending it, but is likely to be sent on to other employees of the network, reverberating, as it were, from computer to computer. So consider this as the electronic equivalent of answering a question at an employee forum. Be crisp and to the point, and your response will help move the thinking of employees toward the desired direction.

I spend some two hours a day reading and responding to messages that come to me from all over the world. I don't generally read them all in one chunk but I almost always make sure that I'm caught up before my day is done. I have found that I can project my thoughts, reactions, biases and preferences very effectively through this means.

Equally important is the opportunity that incoming e-mail gives me to be exposed to the thoughts, reactions, biases and preferences of large numbers of people. More Cassandras bring me news from the periphery this way than through any other means. I witness more arguments, I hear more business gossip, sometimes from people I have never met, than I ever did when I could walk the halls of the one building that housed all Intel employees. What used to be referred to as "managing by walking around" has to a large extent been supplanted by letting your fingers do the walking on your computer keyboard. Given that

Intel has now spread all around the world and I couldn't walk the halls of our sixty-odd buildings even if I spent full time at it, this has become doubly important.

A lot of times, management attempts to communicate a new strategic direction by the medium of closed-circuit television or prerecorded videotape. This may seem like a logical and easy thing to do but it won't work. The interactive element, the give-and-take, the opportunity to ask the "Does it mean that . . ." type of question is lost in this one-way medium. If your employees don't have an opportunity to test your thinking in live sessions or electronically, your message will seem like so much hot air.

Resist the temptation to do what's easy here. Communicating strategic change in an interactive, exposed fashion is not easy. But it is absolutely necessary.

Adjusting to the New

Gordon Moore's comment that half our staff would need to become software types in five years' time was a very valid insight and one that has an equivalent in every company that's struggling with a "10X" force. Simply put, you can't change a company without changing its management. I'm not saying they have to pack up their desks and be replaced. I'm saying that they themselves, every one of them, needs to change to be more in tune with the mandates of the new environment. They may need to go back to school, they may need a new assignment, they may need to spend some years in a foreign post. They need to adapt. If they can't or won't, however, they will need to be replaced with others who are more in tune with the new world the company is heading to.

In our case, we achieved the changes in our management along the lines Gordon suggested. To be sure, some managers left and were replaced by others from within Intel whose backgrounds were much closer to the new requirements. But most of us learned new tricks. For example, as I described, I invested a fair amount of time in learning about the strategies of the software companies in the personal computer industry and establishing relationships with their managers. Others undertook parallel transitions to new assignments. Some even took a step back to a lower-level assignment—a demotion—and, fortified by experiences from which they learned skills that were more appropriate to our new direction, later rose back again in the management ranks. We do this often enough that it is an accepted way for managers to learn the new skills they need as the company heads in a new direction.

Intel isn't alone in exhibiting adaptive behavior. A company that has consistently been able to adapt to new directions over fifty years is Hewlett-Packard. I had the opportunity to see how they go about it. In recent years the management of Hewlett-Packard decided to base their future microprocessor needs on Intel's microprocessor technology. The implication of that was that their computer business, which now uses a microprocessor that they designed themselves, would have to grow to rely on a microprocessor that would be available not just to them but to their competition.

This is a profound change for their business and it had to have been a very hard decision to reach. I witnessed some of the discussions in meetings we had with them, and catching even a glimpse of the process gave me a sense as to why Hewlett-Packard has such a spectacular record of navigating transformations. The discussions were rational, nonthreatening and slow but they steadily moved forward instead of meandering around in circles.

Sometimes management may see the need for a dramatically different new direction but not be able to bring the rest of the company along with them. I have seen a videotape of John Sculley, CEO of Apple Computer from 1983 to 1993, telling a Harvard Business School gathering that two of the biggest mistakes of his career were not adapting Apple's software to Intel's microprocessors and not modifying Apple's then revolutionary laser printer so that it would work with PCs other than those made by Apple. I was stunned when I heard this. Listening to Sculley gave me the impression that he understood the implications of the horizontal industry structure. It appeared that he just wasn't strong enough to overpower Apple's inertia of success that existed because of its fifteen-year history as a fully vertical computer company.

Then there is the intriguing case of Wang Laboratories. Under the leadership of the founder, Dr. An Wang, the company had gone through a tremendous transformation, from being a producer of desktop calculators to becoming a pioneer in distributed word processing systems. Dr. Wang understood these technologies and had an extremely strong hold on his company. His vision was law and his vision was generally spot on. But by 1989, when the PC revolution became truly significant, Dr. Wang was very ill. Without his firm hand at the helm and without senior managers who could step in and define the company's new identity in this time of change, the company lost its strategic direction. This time the company didn't make it through the transformation and actually ended up in Chapter 11 bankruptcy.

Why couldn't Apple and Wang rein in chaos?

It seems that companies that successfully navigate through strategic inflection points have a good dialectic between bottom-up and top-down actions. Bottom-up actions come from the ranks of middle managers, who by the nature of their jobs are exposed to the first whiffs of the winds of change, who are located at the periphery of the action where change is first perceived (remember, snow melts at the periphery) and who therefore catch on early. But, by the nature of their work, they can only affect things locally: The production planners can affect wafer allocation but they can hardly affect marketing strategy. Their actions must meet halfway the actions generated by senior management. While those managers are isolated from the winds of change, once they commit themselves to a new direction, they can affect the strategy of the entire organization.

The best results seem to prevail when bottom-up and top-down actions are equally strong.

We can display this point in the following two-by-two matrix:

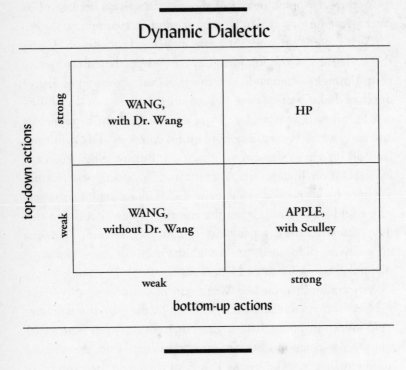

Dynamic Dialectic

The best quadrant to be in is the top right one—strong top-down and strong bottom-up actions roughly balancing.

Dynamic Dialectic

If the actions are dynamic, if top management is able to alternately let chaos reign and then rein in chaos, such a dialectic can be very productive. When top management lets go a little, the bottom-up actions will drive toward chaos by experimenting, by pursuing different product strategies, by generally pulling the company in a multiplicity of directions. After such creative chaos reigns and a direction becomes clear, it is up to senior management to rein in chaos. A pendulum-like swing between the two types of actions is the best way to work your way through a strategic transformation.

This dynamic dialectic is a must. The wisdom to guide a company through the valley of death cannot as a practical matter reside solely in the heads of top management. If senior management is a product of the legacy of the company, its thinking is molded by the old rules. If they are from the outside, chances are they really don't understand the evolving subtleties of the new direction. They must rely on middle management. Yet the burden of guidance also cannot rest solely on the judgment of middle management. They may have the detailed knowledge and the hands-on exposure but by necessity their experience is specialized and their outlook is local, not company-wide.

I learned this lesson the hard way. Intel before the crisis of the mid-1980s had a strategic planning system that was resolutely bottom-up. Middle managers were asked to prepare strategic plans for their areas, then at a detailed and lengthy session they presented their thoughts, strategies, requirements and plans to an assembled group of senior managers. These sessions were very one-way—middle managers did all the work leading to the presentations and they did most of the talking. We senior managers sat on the other side of the table and asked occasional questions, which worked to expose weaknesses of logic and inconsistency in the data. But our questions, which were largely nitpicky, didn't even hint at strategic directions.

These sessions served their purpose as long as the overarching strategy of the company was simply to produce bigger and better semiconductor memories ahead of the competition. They filled in the details: what technology we needed to develop and how we would develop it, what products we would base on these technologies and so on.

But as we began to drift into the strategic inflection point that I described in Chapter 5, the woeful inability of this system to deal with big-time change became sorely evident. How could the middle managers who were responsible for memory products deal with the larger question of "Do we even have a chance in the memory business in the first place?" How could the head of the microprocessor organization raise the basic question, "Was it right for Intel to continue to put our best technology resources on the troubled memory business while starving the emerging microprocessor business?" Senior management needed to step in and make some very tough moves, and ultimately, under the duress of lots of red ink, we did. But we also realized then that there must be a better way to formulate strategy.

What we needed was a balanced interaction between the middle managers, with their deep knowledge but narrow focus, and senior management, whose larger perspective could set a context. The dialectic between these two would often result in searing intellectual debates. But through such debates the shape of the other side of the valley would become clear earlier, making a determined march in its direction more feasible.

An organization that has a culture that can deal with these two phases—debate (chaos reigns) and a determined march (chaos reined in)—is a powerful, adaptive organization.

Such an organization has two attributes:

1. It tolerates and even encourages debate. These debates are vigorous, devoted to exploring issues, indifferent to rank and include individuals of varied backgrounds.

2. It is capable of making and accepting clear decisions, with the entire organization then supporting the decision.

Organizations that have these characteristics are far more strategic-inflection-point-ready than others.

While the description of such a culture is seductively logical, it's not a very easy environment in which to operate, particularly if you are a newcomer to it and are not familiar with the subtle transition in the swings of the pendulum. An example comes to mind. Some time ago we hired a very competent senior manager from outside Intel as part of the process of bringing computer expertise into our management ranks. He seemed to land on his feet, seemed to enjoy the give-and-take characteristic of our environment and diligently tried to follow the workings of the company as he understood them. Yet he missed the essence of what made it really work.

At one point he organized a committee and charged it to investigate an issue and come up with a recommendation. It turned out that this manager knew all along what he wanted to do, but instead of giving that direction to the committee, which he could have, he was hoping to engineer a bottom-up decision to the same effect. When the committee came up with the opposite recommendation, he felt cornered. At this late stage, he tried to dictate his solution to people who by now had spent months struggling with an issue and had firmed up their minds. It just couldn't be done. Coming as it did at this late stage, his dictate seemed utterly arbitrary. The workings of our corporate culture rejected it, and the man had a very hard time understanding where he went wrong.

The Other Side of the Valley

Many companies have gone through strategic inflection points. They are alive, competing, even winning. They have survived the challenges of their valleys of death and have emerged stronger than when they went in.

Hewlett-Packard grew to become a $30 billion company, largely owing to their success in computers. They are second only to IBM in that business.

Intel became the largest semiconductor producer in the world based on a microprocessor-centered strategy. And Intel coming out of the Pentium processor-flaw crisis is stronger than ever and more in tune with its customers.

Next is alive and contributing to the computer industry as a software company.

AT&T and the regional Bell companies thrive, compete and have a market valuation many times what AT&T had before the breakup.

The ports of Singapore and Seattle are thriving.

The Warner Brothers movie studio rode the sound wave to become a major media company.

The other side of the valley of death represents a new industry order that was hard to visualize before the transition. Management did not have a mental map of the new landscape before they encountered it. Getting through the strategic inflection point required enduring a period of confusion, experimentation and chaos, followed by a period of single-minded determination to pursue a new direction toward an initially nebulous goal. It required listening to Cassandras, deliberately fostering debates and constantly articulating the new direction, at first tentatively but more clearly with each repetition. It required casualties and personal transformation; it required accepting the fact that not all would survive and that those who did would not be the same as they had been before.

Beyond a doubt, going through the valley of death that a strategic inflection point represents is one of the most daunting tasks an organization has to endure. But when "10X" forces are upon us, the choice is taking on these changes or accepting an inevitable decline, which is no choice at all.

The Internet: Signal or Noise? Threat or Promise?

''Anything that can affect industries whose total revenue base is many hundreds of billions of dollars is a big deal.''

Netscape went public as I was working on this book. I knew of the company, and I thought that they had a lot of promise. But the way the stock skyrocketed on the first day it was available for public purchase and its continuing growth just blew me away. I could find no obvious rational explanation for this incredibly rapid stock appreciation. Something was going on, beyond merely a promising new company being discovered by a growing number of investors.

Netscape's business premise was completely intertwined with the evolving Internet. And as the stocks of other Internet-based companies also soared in Netscape's wake, it became clear that the investment community's excitement had as much to do with the Internet as with Netscape.

The press was not far behind. An avalanche of long feature articles followed, generally creating a dramatized confrontation between software companies that based their activities on the Internet—typified by Netscape, or sometimes Sun—and the established order, as exemplified by Microsoft.

Something was going on, something was changing. . . .

What Is the Internet Anyway?

For those of you who are not sure what the Internet is but perhaps were afraid to ask, let's backtrack a bit. Simply put, the Internet is networks of computers connected to each other. If you have a personal computer in California and you're connected to the Internet, you can exchange data with other computers connected to the Internet in California, in New York, in Germany or in Hong Kong, sort of like what's shown in the sketch below.

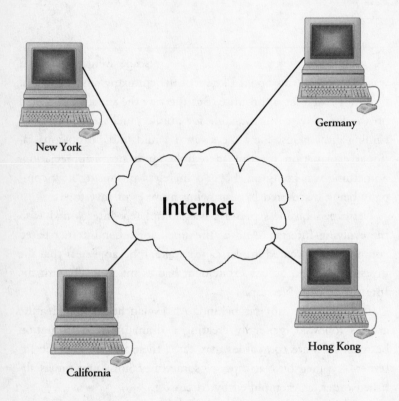

The work leading to the Internet started in the late sixties with government-initiated—and -funded—connections between various big research computers. The idea was to provide a means of communication that could survive a nuclear explosion that might take down the country's ordinary telephone infrastructure. Then other computers started joining in. The Internet kept growing and multiplying as people developed more university networks, corporate networks and government networks, and connected them to all the other previously linked networks. They were motivated by the premise that the more computers are connected to each other, the more useful it is to be connected. I like to think of the interlinked networks of all the computers on the Internet as forming a "connection co-op."

An important element in establishing this "connection co-op" was defining a set of connection rules, so that any network that followed these rules could readily plug into the existing network. I imagine that the evolution of railroad networks in the last century must have followed a similar course. The myriad railroad companies needed to agree on common track gauges. Once they did that, every loop and spur could be connected to the rail networks that spanned the entire United States, and a boxcar could go from California to Kansas, crossing sections of track owned by different companies without a hitch. Similarly, today, a pile of data can originate in California, travel over a number of lines, cross the boundaries of many different networks and arrive at its destination, say, a computer in Kansas. In other words, the Internet provides a universal gauge for computer data.

The growth of this setup of interconnected computer networks has been under way for decades. At first the network served as the means for government and university researchers to communicate with one another. It grew at a moderate pace. Later, the Internet intersected another phenomenon: the mushrooming of personal computers connected to local area networks (LANs).

LANs were a phenomenon unrelated to the Internet. They were a consequence of the proliferation of PCs in corporations and other institutions. At first, PCs were used for individual tasks alone. Increasingly, however, they were connected to each other, first so that they could share an expensive printer, later so that they could exchange data, files and mail. Once large numbers of personal computers at each organization were interconnected through their own local area network, people got the idea that their LAN could be connected to the Internet. When that happened, that corporation's network became part of the "connection co-op." At this time, two phenomena—the growth of the original Internet and the growth of networked PCs—converged, and with the inclusion of corporate LANs, the Internet's growth accelerated enormously.

Not only did the growth rate accelerate but the nature of participants in the Internet also changed. They originally consisted of university researchers sending their studies, papers and data to each other. But as millions of networked personal computers joined the "connection co-op," the Internet became the means for every PC user to become connected to every other PC user.

How could such a complex network keep up with such unbridled growth? It could precisely because of the fact that is a "connection co-op." As each corporation strengthens its own network, it contributes to the strength of the overall network. As in any good co-op, people acting in their own self-interest act in the interests of the whole.

Then there is also a major boost to the carrying capacity from the way the Internet operates. When it was first created, the idea was to provide many alternate routes by which to send data over long-distance telephone lines, so that if one route was blocked or didn't work the system automatically found another one. This is done by large strings of data being broken down into smaller chunks, or packets, which are more easily absorbed into the stream of bits already flowing by. This approach expands the capacity of a network without additional investment. As a rough analogy, consider sending a group of passengers on a trip at the last minute. While it may be impossible for a large group to find a block of airline seats, individual passengers can generally get on board because there are usually a few random, empty places. The airline may even be willing to sell those tickets at a lower price because it doesn't want to fly with empty seats. On the Internet, the packets of data are like passengers sitting in the otherwise empty seats of long-distance telephone networks. They fill the gaps between packets from other users. This method of transmission makes extremely efficient use of the existing telephone networks.

Two additional phenomena further accelerated the growth of the Internet. The first was the fact that personal computers were being improved and upgraded to become multimedia PCs, meaning that they were able to deal with colorful images, photos, sound and even video. The second was that a researcher at CERN (a European nuclear research organization) named Tim Berners-Lee developed a means of linking the data on one computer to the data on any other computer in a way that made it extremely simple for a computer user to perform such a feat. When you clicked on a highlighted key word, such as the name of a company, the connection would automatically be made throughout the entire Internet network, and the computer that contained information about that company would be opened up for your examination. The portion of the Internet that combines colorful graphics with Berners-Lee's search method is the World Wide Web.

To a computer user, the fact that any PC on any person's desk could become a window into millions of computers all over the world was like a miracle. And the fact that the material in those computers could be enhanced with colorful graphics, photographic images and even rudimentary sound and video made it a very seductive miracle.

To sum up, this miracle owed its existence to the confluence of four forces: the ongoing evolution of interconnected networks, the presence of large numbers of personal computers on local area networks that could be connected to the bigger network via a "universal gauge," the spread of multimedia to personal computers and the Berners-Lee search method. Just as a mixture of chemicals consisting of just the right ingredients can undergo spontaneous combustion, this confluence brought about an explosion of public interest in the Internet. But is that explosion a flash in the pan or does it signal the start of a more lasting change?

It so happens that as I was writing this book Intel's semiannual strategic gathering was coming up. My role at these occasions is to describe our business environment as I see it, and to call attention to significant changes. I felt that the Internet was the biggest change in our environment over the last year.

But that feeling was not enough. I needed to deal with the question, Could it be a "10X" force for Intel? If it is, what must we do?

Bits and Stolen Eyeballs

After thinking about it quite a while, I felt that the phenomenon of connecting all the computers in the world has such a wide reach that it would affect a number of industries.

Because it is a communications technology, the Internet is, of course, likely to impact the telecommunications industry. Could it have a "10X" impact? Consider the cost of sending a certain amount of information over the telephone lines. The technology by which data packets are sent through the Internet uses the existing infrastructure so much more efficiently that it is rapidly delivering connection services that can be substantially less expensive than ordinary telephone connections. In other words, the data traffic on the Internet represents a more cost-effective, commodity-like method of connection than a traditional telephone call.

But beyond this it has further efficiencies as people translate an increasing portion of information previously sent by conventional telephony into data. It is a little bit like the way sending a fax compares to reading a document over the telephone; it is more cost-efficient because you can send a lot more information in a shorter period of time. All this suggests the potential to decrease telephone companies' revenues.

But the Internet traffic also represents an extra business opportunity for telephone companies. It can be an opportunity to utilize the monumental investments they have made in building their connectivity infrastructure. This puts the long-distance carriers into a dilemma: Do they embrace the Internet or do they hide from it?

In other words, the Internet has pluses and minuses for the telecommunications industry. In the near term, growth of the use of the Internet may appear to be more of a threat. But in the long term, data rich in pictures, voice and video promise an even larger use of the Internet and therefore new business opportunities. If we put together a balance sheet of the impact of the Internet on the telecommunications industry, it would look something like the following table.

Pros and Cons of the Internet for the Telecommunications Industry

Positives	Negatives
Additional data communications business	Conventional telephony can be replaced by data communications (it takes less traffic)
Utilizes investment made in infrastructure	Telecommunications could be commoditized
Pictures, voice and video mean lots of data (more traffic)	

The Internet has potentially just as much impact on the software industry. It can provide a much, much more efficient way to distribute software. Think about it. Everything that flows on the Internet is a bunch of bits. And software is a bunch of bits. Software is distributed today by the manufacturers to people like you and me by putting those bits on a floppy disk or a CD-ROM, enclosing the disk or CD in a colorful cardboard box and stashing it on the shelf of retail stores much as if it were detergent or cereal.

However, the bits that make up a word processor or a computer game could just as readily be shipped by the manufacturer to your and my computers through the cost-effective method of the Internet. After all, if bits can flow freely from one computer to another, then someone can take pieces of software—even sizable pieces of software—and move them from one computer to another, or from one computer to a million others. No cardboard box and no shelf space are necessary. And no middleman. The whole sales process would clearly be more effective, not to mention how much easier it would be to upgrade or modify the software.

Look at this phenomenon from the standpoint of retailers, who have made a large business out of stocking and selling bits wrapped in those eye-catching boxes. Won't the Internet have the same impact on these stores as the arrival of a Wal-Mart store would on a small-town retailer? This surely feels like a "10X" force.

Another phenomenon affecting the software business is that the Internet provides a brand-new foundation on which software can be designed. This foundation doesn't care about the specific nature of any of the computers connected to the Internet—it works with all kinds of computers. If software—maybe lots of software—can be generated for this new target, won't that siphon off business from Intel and from those computer manufacturers and software developers who have built their businesses around our products? Could it have a "10X" impact on them—and on us?

But again, this is not all. All the media companies are getting caught up in this swirl too. In the past several years practically every media organization—the Viacoms, the Time Warners—has founded "a new media" division for experimentation, much of which is now focused on the World Wide Web. Start-up companies are springing up on both coasts of the United States to service those companies who want to create their own Web site and to measure how many people look at their information as such. Even advertisers are joining in.

This could be an even bigger deal than what is happening to the telecommunications and the personal computing industries. By some estimates, worldwide spending on advertising is some $345 billion dollars. Right now, all of this money is spent on advertising in newspapers, magazines, radio and television. The money flows from advertisers like GM, Coca-Cola and Nike through the conventional media industry without any of it ending up in the pockets of the personal computing or telecommunications industries. That may be about to change.

If I sketch a "before and after" map of the industry, it might look like the figures on the next page.

What this map suggests is that the Internet, or, to be precise, the World Wide Web, is another way for advertisers—the GMs, the Coca-Colas, the Nikes—to reach their consumers with their messages. To do that on a big scale, you have to "steal the eyeballs," so to say, of the consumer audience from where they get those messages today (i.e., newspapers, magazines, radio and television) to displays on the World Wide Web. If this happens to any great extent, it would obviously be a big deal for both the old industries—the newspapers, magazines, radio and television networks—who would lose some of the funds, and also for the new industries—the connection providers, the people involved in generating the World Wide Web, the people who make the computers—who would gain some of those funds. What would be a boon to the latter would clearly be a loss to the former.

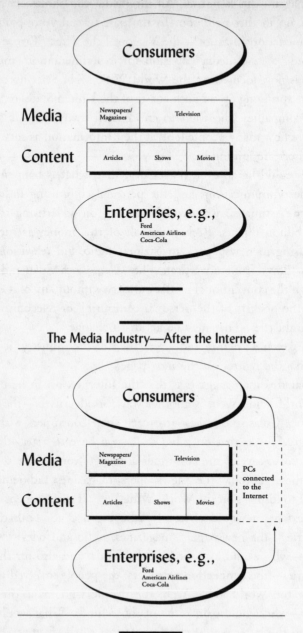

But for this to happen in any big way, lots of eyeballs would have to be lured away from the traditional media. The information on the Internet would need to be made as appealing as the programming on traditional media today. There's a lot of experimentation going on to make computer screens come alive: technology to make objects appear to be three-dimensional, to allow the viewer to move among them as if he were navigating in a room, to enrich the content with good-quality audio and video. All of these improvements could be brought to bear to jazz up the information found on the World Wide Web, so that it would match or even exceed the richness we are already accustomed to on the television screen. And the probability that PC production rates are likely to surpass combined black-and-white and color television production rates in the next year or two lends support to the plausibility that PCs connected by the Internet could, in fact, become a significant alternative to televisions.

Given the size of the media industry, the rewards to the new players would be enormous. Of course, so would be the loss to the traditional media industry—unless, that is, the market expands, reaches more people and therefore benefits all players. We may be witnessing the birth of a new media industry. If that is so, it surely represents a "10X" change!

What About Us?

As I began to prepare my assessment of Intel's business environment for the upcoming meeting, I had lots of things to consider. Clearly, if interconnected computers represented the basis for a new media industry, that could have an enormous positive impact on our business. Much as improved personal productivity in offices drove the growth of our industry in the eighties, sharing data among working individuals continues to propel this growth in the nineties. Becoming a medium for the delivery of commercial messages could continue this growth into the next decade. For this to happen, content has to come to life, objects need to become three-dimensional and sound and video need to become ubiquitous. Processing the large number of bits that make these up requires higher and higher power microprocessors. This has wonderful promise for our business.

But (and there is always a but) if software developed for the Internet will run on anybody's microprocessors, that would open our business to competition by a number of players who today are not really players because their chips don't run the software that personal computer users predominantly use. Our product could be commoditized. And that's not the only threat on the horizon.

A few industry figures have been going around touting the emergence of inexpensive "Internet appliances." These simplified computers would rely on other larger centralized computers someplace on the Internet to store their data and to do much of their number crunching, and would just transmit to the computer users whatever software and data they needed, whenever they needed it. The argument goes that, this way, users would not have to know as much about computing as they do now because all of their tasks would be performed behind the scenes by the network of larger computers. Such an Internet appliance could be built around a simpler and less expensive microchip. Clearly, this would be detrimental to our business.

But there are a number of questions associated with this proposition. The most important is, Is such a computing device even technically feasible? It probably is, but it probably wouldn't do much. Fundamentally, you can't fool Mother Nature in computing, either. Inexpensive microprocessors are usually slow. A simple and cheap microprocessor would not do a wonderful job of creating content that is appealing enough to steal eyeballs. Surely one could make the sort of television sets that prevailed and functioned quite effectively twenty-five years ago for a lot less money than today's TVs cost. But consumers don't want yesterday's capabilities in TVs—or in computers. And consumers may want lower prices but not at the risk of going back technically.

And there is an even more important issue involved. In 1995, some 60 million PCs were bought by consumers. What motivated these purchases? I think most of them were bought for two types of use: first, use that involves the individual user's own data and own applications; and second, use that involves sending and sharing data to and with others, either within a corporate network or through the telephone system. The Internet fosters the emergence of a third class of use: applications and data that are stored at some other computer someplace, prepared and owned by unrelated individuals or organizations, that anyone can access through this pervasive, inexpensive set of connections, the "connection co-op."

While this last category is amazing even as it is today, and probably has great promise going into the future, can it really effectively replace the first two classes of use? I don't think so. I think a *triad* of categories of applications will prevail indefinitely. The beauty and allure of personal computers is the very flexibility with which they can deal with all three categories. A computing device that is useful for only one of these categories would not be attractive in comparison with a computing device that can deal with all three.

As I continued to work up my presentation, I realized it was time to draw up another balance sheet and take stock of all of these applications. I show this balance sheet on the next page.

Threat or Promise?

Before we ask what this balance sheet adds up to, let's ask a more basic question. Is the Internet that big a deal? Or is it an overhyped fad?

I think it *is* that big a deal. I think anything that can affect

Pros and Cons of the Internet for Intel

Positives	Negatives
More applications	Microprocessors could be commoditized
Cheaper connectivity	More intelligence resides on centralized computer
Cheaper software distribution	Internet appliance might make do with a cheap microprocessor
Media business opens up; needs powerful microprocessors	

industries whose total revenue base is many hundreds of billions of dollars is a big deal.

Does it represent a strategic inflection point for Intel? Does it change any of the forces affecting our business, including our complementors, by a "10X" factor?

As I look at the above balance sheet, I don't see that either our customers or our suppliers would be affected in a major way. What about our competition? Let's apply the silver bullet test. Does the Internet bring on the scene players that would be more attractive targets for our silver bullet than the targets we have now? My gut says no. There will be new players on the scene to be sure, but they are just as likely to play the role of complementors as competitors. I certainly wouldn't want to use a silver bullet to take out a complementor that might bring new capabilities to us.

Does my list of fellow travelers change? It does, because companies that used to be complementors to our competitors are now generating software that works as well on computers based on our microchips as on computers based on others. That makes them our complementors too. Also new companies are being created almost daily to take advantage of the opportunity provided by the Internet. Creative energy and funds are pouring in, much of which is going to bring new applications for our chips. So my fellow travelers are likely to grow in number, whereas I don't see that we are about to lose any.

What about our people? Will they be out of it and not "get it?" I don't think that's very likely. A lot of our people have followed the evolution of the Internet from research to mass market both in their capacities as researchers and in their capacities as users of the mass-market version. Their presence ensures that we have the genetic mixture that represents this technology in our midst.

Let's test for dissonance. Are we doing things that are different from what we are saying? We are busily involved in communicating Intel messages on the World Wide Web ourselves. We have ongoing contact with most of the key players in this emerging branch of our business. We even talk with the people who are advocating the development of the inexpensive Internet appliance without an Intel chip in it. I don't see signs of strategic dissonance. But then again, as the CEO, I could very well be the last one to notice.

All this suggests that the Internet is not a strategic inflection point for Intel. But while the classic signs suggest it isn't, the totality of all the changes is so overwhelming that deep down I think it *is*.

What Do We Do?

On balance, I think the promises of the Internet outweigh the threats. Still, we won't harness the opportunity by simply letting things happen to us. Because this "we" specifically includes me, I have to ask, What do I do differently?

I decide to devote more than half of my environmental assessment to the Internet. While that's an easy thing to decide, to fill my presentation with things I'm not embarrassed to say to my colleagues is harder. In other words, I have to study.

I read everything I can lay my hands on. I spend many hours searching out computers located on the World Wide Web and looking at their contents, reading the content of both competitors and oddball presences. I visit other companies, including those that at first blush might be regarded as the enemy because they are devoted to diminishing our business by putting an Internet appliance on the market as a substitute for PCs. I ask our own people to show me things we can do with PCs attached to the Internet.

Gradually, my picture gets clearer. I put my presentation together and finally give it to forty or so of our senior management team, some of whom know a whole lot more about my subject than I do and some of whom haven't given any of it much thought. Comments on my presentation range from "This was the best strategic analysis you've ever done" to "Why the hell did you waste so much time on the Internet?" But I succeed with one thing: the center of gravity of our management discussion shifts measurably.

There seems to be a measure of embarrassment surrounding things to do with the Internet. People know a lot less than they let on. Being familiar with the Internet has become a cultural mandate that causes people to be embarrassed to ask basic questions, so my sense is that a lot of the familiarity that exists is extremely superficial. We set up a hands-on course for our senior managers and for our sales force, where they get to experience the current status of the World Wide Web first-hand. The hope is that this course will fill in the background bit by bit without confronting people with their ignorance point-blank.

I have to admit that my own knowledge is too superficial for my taste as well. But as my knowledge deepens, my conviction is growing that the triad of software coming from personal sources, from telephone and network sources and from the Internet will *together* be what will drive our industry in the years ahead. My conviction is also growing that the media and the advertising industries represent a growing opportunity for us.

We have a few problems in exploiting all this. We need to update our own genetic makeup, to be more in tune with the new environment. We have a whole slew of new fellow travelers that we need to get to know, to cultivate and learn to work with: software companies that we never had anything to do with in the past, telecommunications providers that are in the process of upgrading their networks, advertising and media companies that want to learn about our technology and advertisers who have paid no attention to the computing world until now but suddenly realize that they had better start.

Do we have the time, the attention and the discipline to play this more complex role? We may need to rethink our entire corporate organization structure and modify it to let us play this role with fewer internal complexities. Such a change would touch the lives of thousands of our employees. They would need to understand why we would tinker with what has worked well for us in the past.

Intel operates by following the direction set by three high-level corporate strategic objectives: the first has to do with our microprocessor business; the second with our communications business; the third with our operations and the execution of our plans. We add a fourth objective, encapsulating all the things that are necessary to mobilize our efforts in connection with the Internet. This is preceded by a lot of argument; some think we might just as well fold all the Internet-related things we need to do under the other three objectives. I feel otherwise. Packaging Internet activities separately and elevating them on a par with our other three objectives is a way to communicate their significance to the entire company.

So that's where we are.

Except for one last thing. What if the people who believe in the cheap Internet appliance turn out to be right?

It is likely that the Internet appliance is a case of turning the clock backward, given that the trend over the last twenty to thirty years has consisted of pulling down intelligence from big computers to little ones. I don't believe that the Internet is about to reverse this trend. But then again, my genes were formed by those same twenty or thirty years. And I'm likely to be the last one to know.

So I think there is one more step for Intel to take to prepare ourselves for the future. And I think we should take it now while our market momentum is stronger than ever. I think we should put together a group to build the best inexpensive Internet appliance that can be built, around an Intel microchip. Let this group try to derail our strategies themselves. Let them be our own Cassandras. Let them be the first to tell us whether this can be done and whether what I now think is noise is, in fact, a strong signal that, once again, something has changed.

Career Inflection Points

''Career inflection points caused by a change in the environment do not distinguish between the qualities of the people that they dislodge by their force.''

In 1998, I relinquished my position as Intel's CEO after eleven years in the job. I did this as part of a normal succession process. I have always regarded preparing for succession to be part of a manager's job and have often stated that belief. Now I could do no less than what I expected others to do.

For a number of years, there had been a growing consensus among members of Intel's board of directors about my probable successor. We had often discussed this choice and consequently, over the years, moved the person whom we were considering into positions of increasing responsibility. My change of status was widely expected, both inside and outside the company. I continue to hold the job of chairman, go to work every day and participate in many of the same activities as before. Still, I knew that there would be a difference, and that the difference would grow in time.

As career changes go, this was a mild one, as mild as they come. But it still made me think about the millions of career changes that occur each year around us. Some of them are as natural as mine, but many more occur in adverse circumstances. Consider this: According to some statistics, 1998 will have seen a trillion dollars' worth of merger and acquisition activities. That trillion-dollar figure signifies changes in corporate structure employing perhaps a million people.

There are other forces at work today that further alter the work environment. The Internet tidal wave that I described in Chapter 9 has grown and accelerated, increasingly affecting the way a large number of companies do business. It destroys existing business methods and creates new ones. Many jobs get shaken up in the process.

The year 1998 saw the momentum of the Asian economies go from fast-forward to reverse. Those countries fueled economic growth all over the world with their appetite for new products and services. The repercussion of the changes brought about by the Asian economies' sudden stalling-out has affected an untold number of careers in Asia and the rest of the world.

Clearly, if environmental changes beget strategic inflection points for companies, they do so even more for the careers of the employees of those companies.

Nor are environmental changes the only ones that precipitate upheavals in individual careers. The desire for a different lifestyle, or the fatigue that sets in after many years of doing a stressful job, can cause people to re-evaluate their needs and wants, and can build to a force as powerful as any that comes from the external environment. Put another way, your internal thinking and feeling machinery is as much a part of your environment as an employee as your external situation. Major changes in either can affect your work life.

Are there any lessons from how corporations handle cataclysmic change that can be applied to individual careers?

Your Career Is Your Business

I have long held that each person, whether he is an employee or self-employed, is like an individual business. Your career is literally your business, and you are its CEO. Just like the CEO of a large corporation, you must respond to market forces, head off competitors, take advantage of complementors and be alert to the possibility that what you are doing can be done in a different way. It is your responsibility to protect your career from harm and to position yourself to benefit from changes in the operating environment.

As environmental conditions change, as they inevitably will, the trajectory of this *business of one* undergoes a familiar curve, reaching a defining point where the action of the CEO, i.e., *you*, determines whether your career path bounces upward or accelerates into a decline. In other words, you face a *career inflection point*.

Just as a strategic inflection point marks a crisis point for a business, a career inflection point results from a subtle but profound shift in the operating environment, where the future of your career will be determined by the actions you take in response. While those actions will not necessarily introduce an immediate discontinuity into your career, their impact will unleash forces that, in time, will have a lasting and significant effect. As we have seen, a strategic inflection point reflects a wrenching moment in the life of a company, but the effort of navigating through it is spread around among members of a community. Career inflection points are even more intense for an individual because everything rests on his or her shoulders.

Career inflection points are commonplace. A story comes to mind. It so happens that it was related to me by a business journalist who had interviewed me when this book was first published. This man used to be a banker. He was happily and productively employed until one day he went to work and learned that his employer had been acquired by another, larger bank. In short order he was out of a job. He decided to change careers and become a stockbroker. He knew that he would have to pay his dues. While he was comfortable with financial matters, he knew that a banker's skills are not the same as those required of a stockbroker. So he went to stockbroker school and eventually started working as a full-fledged broker.

For a while, things went well and the future looked promising. However, a short time before we met, on-line brokerage firms started to appear. Several of this man's clients left him, preferring to do their business with low-cost on-line firms. The handwriting was on the wall.

This time, our man decided to make his move early. He had always had an interest in, and aptitude for, writing. Building on the financial knowledge that he had first acquired as a banker, and that was reinforced during his stint as a stockbroker, he found himself a job as a business journalist, a less lucrative position but one less likely to be replaced by technology. At the time we met, his career was in ascendancy. The transition this time was not as traumatic, mainly because he initiated it in his own time, unlike the previous time, when the change was initiated for him by outside circumstances.

A lot of the elements involved in dealing with strategic inflection points are at play here, too. The most important—and the most difficult—is to be alert to changes in your environment. When you work inside an organization, you're often sheltered from a lot of things going on in the world at large that are relevant to the health of the business you work for. When you got this job, even though deep down you knew it was unlikely to be what you would do for the rest of your work life, you may very well have tacitly relinquished responsibility for your welfare to your employer. But by taking your eyes off the environment in which your company operates, like the CEO of a large organization, you too may be the last to know of potential changes that could have an impact on your career.

How do you get around that?

The Mental Fire Drill

Tune your alarm system to be more alert to potential strategic inflection points in businesses like yours. Go through a mental fire drill in anticipation of the time when you may have a real fire on your hands. Simply put, be a little paranoid about your career.

Put yourself in the shoes of the CEO of a large company. You must open up your mind to outside views and stimuli. Read the newspapers. Attend industry conferences. Network with your colleagues in other companies. You may hear anecdotal descriptions of changes that may be relevant to you before they add up to a cogent trend. Listen to chatter from colleagues and friends.

In a corporation, the helpful Cassandras would be the front-line employees who sense potential changes first and bring early tidings of strategic inflection points to the CEO. In the case of a career inflection point, the Cassandras are likely to be concerned friends or family members who work in a different industry or competitive environment and deduce winds of change that you don't sense yet. Perhaps they have already been bounced around by a wave of change that's coming your way. Or perhaps they've experienced a career inflection point in their own industry and have a lesson to impart, even if they're not in your line of work.

When different sources—newspaper stories, industry scuttlebutt and company gossip—and your Cassandras all reinforce each other, it is really time to sit up and take notice.

Put yourself in the picture. Ask yourself a series of questions:

- Do these anecdotes indicate changes that might somehow apply to you?
- How would an important change manifest itself in your situation?
- Would you know about such changes from the kind of business information that you routinely get from your company?

- Would you be able to predict that changes like this are coming your way from your company's financial performance?
- Can you bring up your concerns with your boss?
- What would you do if you were affected by such a change?
- How likely is your company to be affected by changes in your industry?
- Would those industry changes be a temporary setback for your company or a harbinger of a longer-term industry restructuring? The distinction is important because your company can bounce back from the former with no effect on your career; the latter, however, will likely have a lasting impact on it.
- Consider how developments originating in other industries might have a ripple effect on your job. When a new machine or a new computer system comes in, can it change the way your department does its work? Are your skills as good in doing things with this new technique as they were before? Are you confident of learning the new ways? If not, what should you do?
- Maybe your company is losing ground to a competitor. What does that imply? Could you be in the right line of work but working for the wrong employer? Or is the entire industry shifting ground? Asking and answering such questions are important because the measures you take to fix things vary with the circumstances. If your employer is losing out to another outfit, you could continue to utilize your skills and just look for a way to jump from the sinking ship to one more likely to navigate the competitive seas successfully. On the other hand, when there's a fundamental change in the industry and you don't change your skills, you will lose at both winning companies and losing companies. That is a situation that can truly be classified as a career inflection point.

The existence of career inflection points is best analyzed by conducting a vigorous debate with sympathetic associates. You need to cultivate the habit of constantly questioning your work situation. By examining the tacit assumptions underlying your daily work, you will hone your ability to recognize and analyze change. In other words, get into the habit of conducting an internal debate about your work environment *with yourself.*

Timing Is Everything

As with strategic inflection points of the business kind, success in navigating a career inflection point depends on a sense of timing. Are you picking up on the portents that something may be changing? Have you already anticipated a change and prepared for it? Or are you waiting until the signs are incontrovertibly clear before you make your move?

The stages of dealing with a career inflection point, if anything, are even more emotion-laden than with inflection points affecting a company. Little wonder; after all, you are likely to have invested a lot in getting your career to where it is. More important, you've invested your hopes in the further upward trajectory of your career. As signs appear that the curvature is shifting downward, your whole being will work at trying to deny that this is so.

Often you'll be tempted to believe that because of your particular individual excellence, you'll be exempt from the change. You'll think, "It may happen to others but not to me." This is a dangerous conceit. It's the equivalent of the "inertia of success" that dogs companies which have done well. Career inflection points caused by a change in the environment do not distinguish between the qualities of the people that they dislodge by their force.

History offers plenty of examples. In early nineteenth-century England, the increasing use of mechanized looms made woven cloth so much more cheaply than by traditional manual means that an entire class of craftsmen, both expert and mediocre weavers, lost their independent livelihoods and were forced to work as unskilled laborers in the mills. The rise of the automobile threw harnessmakers, both good and bad, out of work. Today, small farmers are struggling to retain their economic viability against competition from agricultural conglomerates. No one is immune to these environmental changes, no matter how skilled and how invulnerable he or she may feel.

Denial can come from two wholly different sources. If you've been very successful in your career, the inertia of success may keep you from recognizing danger. If you've just been hanging on, fear of change and fear of giving up whatever you *have* achieved may contribute to your reluctance to recognize the situation. Either way, denial will cost you time and cause you to miss the optimal moment for action at or near the inflection point.

As in managing businesses, it is rare that people make career calls early. Most of the time, as you look back, you will wish you had made the change earlier. In reality, a change made under the benign bubble of an existing job, when things are still going well, will be far less wrenching than the same change made once your career has started its decline.

Furthermore, if you are among the first to take advantage of a career inflection point, you are likely to find the best pick of the opportunities in your new activity. Simply put, the early bird gets the worm; latecomers will get only the leftovers.

Get in Shape for Change

The time period from an early sense of foreboding to a career inflection point is valuable. Just as athletes get in shape for competition, this is your time to get in shape for change. Picture yourself in different roles. Read about these roles. Talk to people who are in them. Ask yourself questions about them. Conduct a dialogue with yourself about how you suit those roles. Train your brain in preparation for the big change.

Experimentation is a key way to prepare for change. The banker/stockbroker started on his transition to business journalism while he was still employed as a stockbroker. This served several purposes. He dusted off his writing skills, tested the feasibility and practicality of his future change and established contact with potential sources of business before giving up on his main source of income. In doing so, he verified that he could plausibly make a living by writing if he devoted himself to it full-time.

Experimentation can take different forms. It can be moonlighting on a second job, as in this case. It can be going back to school part-time. Or it can be by asking your current employer for a new and entirely different assignment. All are ways to explore new directions for your career and get you ready for a career inflection point.

As you experiment, avoid random motion. Don't just take blind steps in directions whose only common characteristic is that they are different from what you are presently doing. Guide yourself by your knowledge and understanding of the nature of the changes that are upon you; in this way, the experimentation propels you forward in a direction that gets you out of the way of those changes. Look for something that allows you to use your knowledge or skills in a position that's more immune to the wave of changes you have spotted. (Better yet, look for a job that takes advantage of the changes in the first place. Go with the flow rather than fight it.)

It is very important to visualize what you want to achieve before you start to traverse the career equivalent of the valley of death. Ask yourself another set of questions:

- What do you think the nature of your industry is going to be in two or three years?
- Is this an industry you want to be a part of?
- Is your employer in a good position to succeed in this industry?
- What skills do you need to progress in your career in this new landscape?

- Do you have a role model of the person who has the career today that you want to achieve?

Remember the incident I described in Chapter 8, when our then-chairman, Gordon Moore, made a comment to the effect that if we were to change from a semiconductor company to a microprocessor company, half of our management would have to become software types. That observation captured the essence of a strategic change in the workings of the company that, in turn, precipitated career inflection points for quite a few people, including myself. But it also gave us an idea of, if not a role model for, what we would have to learn and how we would have to change.

Much as conducting a dialogue with yourself will help clarify the existence of a career inflection point, an ongoing dialogue about the nature of the future you are headed into will help focus your efforts and allow you to move forward in a number of small, consistent steps rather than in a cataclysmic leap forced on you by the external world.

There are two things that will help you get through the career valley: clarity and conviction. *Clarity* refers to a tangible and precise view of where you're heading with your career: knowing what you'd like your career to be as well as knowing what you'd like your career *not* to be. *Conviction* refers to your determination to get across this career valley and emerge on the other side in a position that meets the criteria you have determined.

When a corporation crosses the valley of death involved in navigating a strategic inflection point, the CEO is called upon to describe a clear vision of the new industry map and provide the leadership to get the organization across this valley. As CEO of your own career, you will have to supply both the vision and commitment yourself. Both are daunting. Arriving at the clarity of direction through a dialogue with yourself and maintaining your conviction when you wake up in the middle of the night filled with doubts are both tough. Yet you have no choice. Inaction will leave you in a position where the action will be forced upon you.

As a single individual, you have just one career. Your best chance to succeed in a career inflection point is to take control of it with full focus and energy, and with no wavering.

You have to steel yourself to recognize that it will take a while before you rebuild your career support system, experience and confidence to the same level that you had before. Part of the support system you will miss is the identity—a brand—your employer gave you. Whether you join another company or go out on your own, you have to let go of one identity and build a new one. This takes effort and time, and most certainly will test your courage. But it will also give you a sense of independence and self-confidence, which will help you in dealing with the inevitable *next* career inflection point.

A New World

Going through a career inflection point is not an easy process. It is not without many dangers. It calls upon all your best resources. It calls upon your understanding of the new world that you wish to become part of, your determination to take control of your career, your ability to adapt your skills to that new world and your resolve as you deal with the fear and anxiety of change.

It's a bit like emigrating to a new country. You pack up and leave an environment you're familiar with, where you know the language, the culture, the people, and where you've been able to predict how things, both good and bad, happen. You move to a new land with new habits, a new language and a new set of dangers and uncertainties.

At times like this, looking back may be tempting, but it's terribly counterproductive. Don't bemoan the way things were. They will never be that way again. Pour your energy, every bit of it, into adapting to your new world, into learning the skills you need to prosper in it and into shaping it around you. Whereas the old land presented limited opportunity or none at all, the new land enables you to have a future whose rewards are worth all the risks.

Notes

Chapter 1: Something Changed

p. 11. "growing at around 30 percent per year . . .": From 1986 to 1994, Intel grew at a 31.3 percent CAGR. *Intel Annual Report,* 1994.

p. 13. "headlines . . .": *New York Times,* November 24, 1994; p. D1; *Wall Street Journal,* December 14, 1994; p. B1.

p. 21. "long-standing bugs . . .": "Attempting to address the complaints of Macintosh users, Microsoft Corp. last week shipped a maintenance release of its best-selling word processing software. The company says the release improves speed and resolves conflicts with a handful of system extensions." "Microsoft Fixes Word for Mac," *ComputerWorld,* March 27, 1995, p. 40. "Apple Computer Inc. joined rival Microsoft Corp. last week by delaying the release of the next major revision of its operating system. Apple's Copland is now expected to ship in mid-1996, not in the middle of 1995 as previously announced." "Microsoft Not Alone: Apple Delays Copland OS Release," *PC Week,* December 26, 1994/January 2, 1995, p. 106. " 'We regret that customers have had incompatibility problems and we are 100% committed to customer satisfaction,' says Steve McBeth, president of Disney Interactive, the company's software arm. 'We won't be satisfied until all compatibility problems are removed.' . . . As company officials now concede, the program was marketed with known errors, wrongly believed to affect only a minute percentage of computers." "A Jungle Out There: The Movie Was a Hit, the CD-ROM a Dud," *Wall Street Journal,* January 23, 1995, p. A1. "Hoping to avert a major revolt, Intuit Inc. last week made available on-line free revised versions of tax preparation software, designed to fix three bugs. . . . Intuit will pay IRS penalties and interest for any errors caused by the bugs, which the company claims affect fewer than 1 percent of MacInTax and TurboTax users." "Intuit Issues Patches for TurboTax and MacInTax," *PC Week,* March 6, 1995, p. 3.

Chapter 2: A "10X" Change

p. 27. "competitive strategy analysis . . .": Michael Porter, *Competitive Strategy: Techniques for Analyzing Industries and Competitors* (New York: The Free Press, 1980), pp. 3–4.

p. 29. "the force of complementors . . .": Adam M. Brandenburger and Barry J. Nalebuff, "The Right Game: Use Game Theory to Shape Strategy," *Harvard Business Review,* July/August 1995, p. 60.

Chapter 3: The Morphing of the Computer Industry

p. 39. "a cost-effectiveness that was easily ten times greater . . .": "In a little over five years, the cost adjusted by performance decreased by 90%. This unprecedented rate of decline in cost to the consumer came about, basically, as a result of standardization. In the future, the price/performance characteristics will continue to drop further and further at this hair-raising rate." Andrew S. Grove, "The Future of the Computer Industry," *California Management Review,* Vol. 33, No. 1, Fall 1990, p. 149.

p. 43. "the way computing was done changed . . .": "Right now the computer business is in a painful transition between two worlds: from the old world of slow-moving, highly integrated systems to the new world of quickly developed, extremely cost-efficient, but not-very-well-integrated technology. . . . The very structure of the industry is being dramatically reshaped by the standardization of the PC." "PCs Trudge Out of the Valley of Death," *Wall Street Journal,* January 18, 1993, p. A10.

p. 43. "big-time computing increasingly started to be done this way . . .": "Within a few years, every computer in the NCR line from PCs on up will be based on one or more Intel microchips. Gone will be NCR's mainframe proprietary designs and any other machine that cannot run standard software. . . ." "Rethinking the Computer: With Superchips, the Network Is the Computer," *Business Week,* November 26, 1990, p. 117.

p. 45. "IBM . . . a $100 billion company . . .": "When Opel

retired as CEO in 1985, the corporation's outlook called for revenue of $100 billion in 1990 and $185 billion by 1994." "The Transformation of IBM," *Harvard Business School Case,* 9-391-073, rev. September 9, 1991, p. 6.

p. 45. Compaq: "Compaq made corporate history by becoming the first company to surpass the billion dollar milestone in sales after only five years of operations." *Compaq 1988 Annual Report,* p. 3.

p. 46. "those that win inevitably get stronger . . .": W. Brian Arthur paraphrases Alfred Marshall's 1890 observation, "If firms' production costs fall as their market shares increase, a firm that simply by good fortune gained a high proportion of the market early on would be able to best its rivals. . . ." The more contemporary version of this theory is summed up by Professor Arthur: "Technologies typically improve as more people adopt them and firms gain experience that guides further development. This link is a positive-feedback loop; the more people adopt a technology, the more it improves and the more attractive it is for further adoption." W. Brian Arthur, *Increasing Returns and Path Dependence in the Economy* (Ann Arbor: University of Michigan Press, 1994), pp. 2, 10.

p. 46. "IBM's growth slowed down . . .": "But [IBM's] PC revenues haven't compensated for a slowdown in mainframes and minis—a slowdown caused in large part by the success of the PC. As a result, IBM's revenue growth has averaged 6.5% since 1984." "Is the Computer Business Maturing? New Technology May Not Halt an Erosion in Growth and Margins," *Business Week,* March 6, 1989, p. 69.

p. 47. "OS/2 worked only on PS/2 computers . . .": "[The new software] will use the IBM Personal System/2 PC as the window into information. . . . [It] requires a new IBM proprietary version of OS/2, the PC operating system, or basic software, introduced two years ago. . . ." "A Bold Move in Mainframes: IBM Plans to Make Them Key to Networking—And So Restore Its Growth: The Software That Ties It All Together," *Business Week,* May 29, 1989, pp. 74–75.

p. 47. "marketing their operating systems to . . . their competitors . . .": "IBM stresses that it will 'open up' OS/2 version 2.0 to companies that don't sell IBM-manufactured PCs. . . . By selling beyond its own confines, IBM—which is responsible for OS/2 version 2.0

development and sales—will help spur interest in the operating system." "IBM Announces OS/2—Again," *Systems Integration,* June 1991, p. 38.

p. 48. "eventually they even passed IBM . . .": In 1994, Compaq shipped 4.8 million units worldwide, compared to IBM's 4.0 million. "Personal Computers Worldwide," *Dataquest,* June 26, 1995, p. 90.

p. 48. "Michael Dell started supplying his friends . . .": "Dell's roots can be traced to a small dorm room at the University of Texas. In 1984, during his freshman year, Michael Dell began buying excess computers from a local retailer, enhancing their features and selling the PCs directly to end users at a discount. In less than a year, Michael was grossing $50,000 a month with his direct relationship marketing approach. He left the University to devote his full attention to his rapidly expanding company, PCs Limited. . . ." "The Story of Dell's Success" from Dell's Home Page on the World Wide Web, June 9, 1995.

p. 49. "Dell . . . is doing about $5 billion worth of business a year . . .": Expected FY96 sales are $4.8 billion. *Bear Stearns Analyst Report,* May 26, 1995.

p. 50. "In adapting, Unisys . . .": "The economic model and the business model of the business we had been in totally changed. So we had to step back and say, well, that means, first of all, we shouldn't be doing things that aren't really of added value to the client. . . . So it's a very different strategy and our success will come from building successful partnerships with our clients, to assist them with information management to get that competitive advantage. . . . If you look at it from revenue streams, [five years from now] you're going to see well over half of the revenue coming from software services and much less coming from hardware." From an interview with Unisys chairman and CEO James Unruh, "Smooth Sailing on an Ink-Black Sea: Unisys Eyes Information Services," *Computer Reseller News,* June 13, 1994, p. 226.

p. 50. "Ray Noorda often tells the story . . .": "Note on the PC Network Software Industry 1990," *Harvard Business School Case* N9-792-022, rev. September 5, 1991, p. 5.

p. 51. failure of "a better PC": For an example, see the story of Digital's Rainbow in Glenn Rifkin and George Harrar, *The Ultimate Entrepreneur: The Story of Ken Olsen and Digital Equipment Corporation* (Chicago: Contemporary Books, 1983), pp. 203–42.

p. 56. "Wal-Mart . . . is competition . . .": "Electronic scanning of the Uniform Product Code (UPC) at the point of sale began in Wal-Mart stores in 1983. . . . Electronic scanning and the need for improved communication between stores, distribution centers, and the head office in Bentonville, Arkansas, led to the investment in a satellite system. . . . Wal-Mart's two-step hub-and-spoke distribution network started with a Wal-Mart truck-tractor bringing the merchandise into a distribution center, where it was sorted for delivery to a Wal-Mart store—usually within 48 hours of the original request." "Wal*Mart Stores, Inc.," *Harvard Business School Case* N9-794-024, rev. April 26, 1994, pp. 6–7.

p. 57. "once Wal-Mart moves to town . . .": "Few local merchants can compete against sprawling 50,000-square-foot stores whose notions counters alone dwarf many rural mom and pop concerns. Nor can many match Wal-Mart's direct-from-factory prices, which are often cheaper than the wholesale prices local shopkeepers pay for their merchandise. As a result, down-town business districts begin to empty, leaving fewer sponsors for Little League teams and a smaller pool of advertisers for the high-school yearbook. 'When Wal-Mart comes in, something has to go out,' observes Rex Campbell, professor of rural sociology at the University of Missouri." "How Wal-Mart Hits Main St.: Shopkeepers Find the Nation's No. 3 Retailer Tough to Beat," *U.S. News and World Report*, March 13, 1989, p. 53.

p. 57. "category killer" strategy: "A significant type of specialty chain that evolved during the 1980s was the 'category killer.' Modeled after Toys "Я" Us, category killers were single-line stores with in-depth inventories in such areas as sporting goods, office supplies, and electronics." Sandra S. Vance and Roy V. Scott, *Wal*Mart: A History of Sam Walton's Retail Phenomenon* (New York: Twayne Publishers, 1994), p. 86.

p. 57. Staples: "To get to know its customers, Staples has been compiling lots of information about buying habits and storing it in a massive database. . . . Staples uses this knowledge to locate new stores where they will be convenient for their customers—such as in neighbor-hoods with lots of law offices. . . . Staples wants to do everything it can to get its best customers coming back to its stores. Since the data-base knows who those folks are, Staples can try to win their loyalty by offering them special discounts." "How One Red-Hot Retailer Wins Customers Loyalty," *Fortune,* July 10, 1995, p. 74.

p. 57. "provide an environment . . .": "B&N [Barnes & Noble] has opened six outlets in the area, including a 35,000-square-foot store stocked with 125,000 titles that opened last fall less than two miles from the Tattered Cover. . . . [T]o fight back, [the Tattered Cover] has extended hours, added a coffee bar, and opened a 7,500-square-foot satellite store in downtown Denver. Next month, [they'll] open a restau-rant atop the flagship store, which is adjacent to Denver's elegant Cherry Creek Shopping Center. So far, however, [they] refuse to dis-count." "Chain-store Massacre in Bookland?" *Business Week,* February 27, 1995, p. 20D.

p. 59. "Next was in financial difficulties . . .": "The company that only two years earlier had gotten an infusion of $100MM from Canon was once again out of money." Randall E. Stross, *Steve Jobs and the Next Big Thing* (New York: Atheneum, 1993), p. 301.

p. 60. "Next, the software company . . .": "Obsessed for years with hardware, Jobs, 37, now recognizes that Next's 'crown jewel' is not its sleek computer but its operating system—[the] software it comes with. . . . So now Jobs is making a bold and desperate move to save Next by transforming it into a publisher of software that runs on other companies' computers." "Steve Jobs' Next Big Gamble," *Fortune,* Feb-ruary 8, 1993, pp. 99–100.

p. 61. Charlie Chaplin's reaction to sound: "Early in 1931 he had made several statements to the press: 'I give the talkies six months more. At the most a year. Then they're done.' Three months later, in May 1931, he had modified his opinion slightly: 'Dialogue may or may not have a place in comedy. . . . What I merely said was that dialogue does not have a place in the sort of comedies I make. . . . For myself I know that I cannot use dialogue.' " David Robinson, *Chaplin: His Life and Art* (New York: McGraw Hill, 1985), p. 465.

p. 61. *"Anna Christie . . .* was both a critical and commercial success . . .": Barry Paris, *Garbo: A Biography* (New York: Alfred A. Knopf, 1995), p. 194.

p. 62. "a '10X' change in the productivity of shipping . . .": "[T]he conventional system eventually came to be associated with relentless increases in cargo handling costs. . . . When expressed in 1870 prices there was a sixteen-fold increase in [loading] costs [between 1870 and 1975]." *The Shipping Revolution: The Modern Merchant Ship,* Conway's History of the Ship (London: Conway Maritime Press, 1992), pp. 42–43.

p. 62. "a worldwide reordering of shipping ports . . .": "[In 1959, the Port of Seattle] was the subject of countless hand-wringing editorials that proclaimed the obvious—it was dying. The Port altered course and became one of the most dynamic ports in the country; the unquestioned leading port north of Oakland, and the sixth busiest container port in the world." Padraic Burke and Dick Paetzke, *Pioneers and Partnerships: A History of the Port of Seattle* (Port of Seattle, 1995), p. 85. "Singapore, for the past five years the world's busiest port, has now surpassed Hong Kong as the world's busiest container port." "New Hub in Southeast Asia: Singapore Manages to Supplant Hong Kong as the World's Number One Container Port," *American Shipper,* June 1991, p. 93. "The marine terminals of New York have been eclipsed since the 1960s by those on the New Jersey side of the harbor, which are better equipped for modern shipping because they have more land and easier access to railways and highways. Government-owned terminals in Manhattan, Brooklyn and Staten Island have been unable to keep up, losing about $40 million annually in the last two years, with little prospect of breaking even in the near future." "Questioning the Viability of New York in Shipping," *New York Times,* August 30, 1995, p. A16.

p. 62. "ports that didn't adopt . . .": "San Francisco does barely 10% of the shipping trade of Seattle, Oakland or Los Angeles. . . . What happened here (in San Francisco) started nearly 30 years ago, with the advent of containerized cargo. . . . [W]hen goods were sealed in large metal containers, uniform in size, easily loaded onto trucks or rail cars, the finger piers were obsolete, and San Francisco became a shipping cemetery. . . . During the 1960s, the shipping repair business employed 20,000 people in San Francisco. Today, barely 500 work on dry-dock operations here." "Past and Future Collide on San Francisco's Waterfront," *New York Times,* February 10, 1995, p. A8.

p. 64. "modified their strategies to take advantage . . .": "[NCR's] System 3000 line, based on Intel Corp.'s 80×86 microprocessors, reaches from portable and pen-based computers; to desktop PCs and workstations; to servers and mainframe-class, parallel-processor computers." "NCR/AT&T: One Era Ends . . . Another Begins," *Electronic Business,* May 1993, p. 37. "H-P, once a nonfactor in the PC business, is now streamlined, nimble, and growing faster than market leader Compaq." "Hewlett-Packard: The Next PC Power," *Fortune,* May 1, 1995, p. 20.

p. 64. DEC and PCs: See Rifkin and Harrar, *The Ultimate Entrepreneur,* p. 242.

p. 64. "Digital broke into the world of computers . . .": "In late 1962, DEC won its breakthrough order. International Telephone and Telegraph bought fifteen PDP-1s to control its message switching systems. This order gave Digital the confidence and financial ability to become a general systems supplier." *Ibid.,* p. 44.

p. 64. "IBM . . . blamed weakness in the worldwide economy . . .": "IBM executives blame their financial performance on other factors, which are beyond their control. Foremost among them: U.S. capital spending patterns, which Akers and his lieutenants say have been disrupted by tax reform." "Computers: When Will the Slump End?" *Business Week,* April 21, 1986, p. 63. "We have this sparkling product line. . . . And we do have an economic environment that has resulted in customers' delaying and deferring decisions. That can't go on forever." Interview with John Akers, *Fortune,* July 15, 1991, p. 43.

p. 65. "Chen described his switch . . .": "Steve Chen, the reclusive supercomputer designer whose last company folded two years ago, has resurfaced with a new firm that embraces a technology approach he once shunned." "Supercomputing's Steve Chen Resurfaces in New Firm," *Reuters,* June 27, 1995.

p. 65. "an analysis of the history of business failures . . .": "Bad things happen to good companies for three reasons: Firms leave their markets, markets escape from firms or both happen simultaneously."

Comments by Richard S. Tedlow in a seminar at Intel, October 7, 1993.

p. 65. Young people's comfort with computers: "63 percent of children ages 11–17 would rather use a computer than read a book; 59 percent would rather use it than watch TV." *San Jose Mercury News,* April 10, 1995, p. 1A.

p. 66. Ford: "In an industry in which market share has always been a key to profitability, every other automobile sold in the United States in 1921 was a Model T." Richard S. Tedlow, *New and Improved: The Story of Mass Marketing in America* (New York: Basic Books, 1990), p. 150.

p. 66. "Alfred Sloan . . . saw a market . . .": " 'The changes in the new model should be so novel and attractive as to create demand for the new value and, so to speak, create a certain amount of dissatisfaction with past models as compared with the new one.' " Alfred Sloan, quoted, *ibid.,* p. 168.

p. 66. "General Motors had taken the lead . . .": "General Motors surpassed Ford in terms of both profit and market share in the 1920s and outperformed Ford in profit every year from 1925 until 1986." *Ibid.,* p. 171.

p. 68. "Cray . . . unable to maintain operations . . .": "In a bitter final chapter signifying the decline of the supercomputer industry and the fortunes of its founding father, computer pioneer Seymour Cray said Friday that his company, Cray Computer Corp. was seeking Chapter 11 bankruptcy protection after failing to raise an additional $20 million to continue operations." *San Jose Mercury News,* March 25, 1995, p. 2D.

p. 69. "airlines . . . place a cap on commissions . . .": "Delta, staggered by its bloated costs, said it made the move as part of its plans to eliminate $400 million in marketing expenses, and $2 billion overall, by 1997. 'It took a lot of nerve to do this,' said Vincent F. Caminiti, Delta's vice president of sales." "Delta Caps Its Commission on Ticket Sales: End of Fixed 10% Fee Aims to Cut Costs but Risks Angering Travel Agents," *Wall Street Journal,* February 10, 1995, p. A2.

p. 69. "agencies instituted a policy of charging customers . . .": "American Express Travel, the country's largest agency, said last week it will charge $20 a ticket on domestic flights costing less than $300 and credit the fee toward cruises or tour packages. Carlson Wagonlit, the No. 2 agency, will charge a $15 fee to first-time customers who travel alone and book no other services." "Coffee, Tea and Fees," *Time,* February 27, 1995, p. 47.

p. 69. "40 percent of all agencies might go out of business . . .": "The American Society of Travel Agents said in a preliminary estimate that as many as 10,000 of its 25,000 members could be put out of business." *Ibid.,* p. 47.

p. 72. For the impact of the 1906 Food and Drugs Act on patent medicines and the pharmaceutical industry, see James Harvey Young, *Pure Food: Securing the Federal Food and Drugs Act of 1906* (Princeton, NJ: Princeton University Press, 1989).

p. 73. "the phone company could not require the use of its own equipment . . .": "In 1968, in a landmark decision known as *Carterfone,* the Federal Communications Commission . . . had ruled that the 'terminal equipment' market should be opened up for the first time to companies other than AT&T. . . . [The FCC] decided that independent companies making new communications devices like answering machines and mobile radio phones should be allowed to interconnect with AT&T's switched phone network, a privilege that had been previously denied to them. Suddenly, phone users could buy non-AT&T equipment and plug it into the telephone lines at their homes or business." Steve Coll, *The Deal of the Century: The Breakup of AT&T* (New York: Atheneum, 1986), pp. 10–11.

p. 73. "the U.S. Government . . . brought suit . . .": "On March 6, 1974, MCI filed a sweeping antitrust suit against AT&T seeking hundreds of millions of dollars in damages. . . . On Wednesday, November 20, 1974 . . . on the fifth floor of the main Justice building at 10th and Pennsylvania, the attorney general met with several antitrust division lawyers to discuss the AT&T case. . . . Shortly before eleven . . . the AT&T lawyers arrived. . . . [The lead lawyer] retained by AT&T stood up to begin AT&T's presentation. . . . [He] began puffing on a pipe [and addressed the attorney general], 'Before we start our presentation, I'd like to know exactly what your state of mind is on this case.' . . . [The attorney general replied] 'I intend to bring action against you.'" *Ibid.,* pp. 52, 65, 67–68.

p. 73. the breakup of the Bell System: "Once again, in 1974, the Justice Department sued AT&T. . . . After dragging on for nearly eight years, the suit was settled by consent decree in January, 1982. AT&T agreed to divest itself of its 22 operating companies, while retaining Western Electric, Bell Labs, and long-distance communications. . . . Judge Greene [later] issued his Modified Final Judgment (MFJ). . . . Under the MFJ, the 22 Bell operating companies were reorganized into seven Regional Holding Companies. . . ." "AT&T and the Regional Bell Holding Companies," *Harvard Business School Case* N2-388-078, rev. March, 1989, pp. 3–4.

p. 74. "long-distance market . . .":

AT&T	60%
MCI	20%
Sprint	10%
LDDS	3%
Wiltel	1%
Other	6%

Arsen Darney and Marlita Reddy, *Share Reporter: An Annual Compilation of Reported Market Share Data on Companies, Products and Services.* Table 1216, p. 318.

p. 74. "a cable network . . .": In 1993, 57 million homes (61.4 percent) had cable. *Statistical Abstract of the United States 1994,* U.S. Department of Commerce, issued September 1994, Washington, D.C. Table 882, p. 567.

pp. 75–76. Deutsche Telekom: "Mr. Sommer is expected to bring to Telekom a global business outlook and a feel for the hotly competitive world of consumer electronics." "Deutsche Telekom Picks Ron Sommer as Its Chairman," *Wall Street Journal,* March 30, 1995, p. B4.

p. 77. AT&T and the Bell companies' combined valuation. In December 1993, following the breakup, AT&T and its successor companies had an approximate market valuation of $60 billion. *Capital International Perspective* (Capital International S.A., Geneva, Switzerland), January 1984, pp. 330–32. In 1995, their market value was approximately $240 billion. *The Red Herring,* September 1995, pp. 110, 112.

Chapter 5: "Why Not Do It Ourselves?"

p. 87. "the 10% rule . . .": Andrew S. Grove, "The Future of the Computer Industry," *California Management Review,* Vol. 33, No. 1, Fall 1990, p. 153.

p. 87. "get '2X' the price of Japanese memories": " 'The DRAM manager would say: With this approach we'll be able to get a price of '2X' that of a standard DRAM, but unfortunately, we just didn't like the 'X.' " "Implementing the DRAM Decision," *Graduate School of Business,* Stanford University, PS-BP-256B, 1991, p. 1.

p. 96. Intel's "public statements . . .": Note the evolution of the phrasing: "Intel is a manufacturer of electronic 'building blocks' used by Original Equipment Manufacturers (OEMs) to construct their systems." *1985 Intel Annual Report,* p. 4. "Intel designs and manufactures semiconductor components and related single-board computers, microcomputer systems and software for original equipment manufacturers." *1986 Intel Annual Report,* p. 4. "The company originally flourished as a supplier of semiconductor memory for mainframe computers and minicomputers. Over time, though, the face of computing, and Intel, have changed. Microcomputers are now the largest, fastest-growing segment of computing, and Intel is a leading supplier of microcomputers." *1987 Intel Annual Report,* p. 4.

Chapter 6: "Signal" or "Noise"?

p. 104. "an auxiliary one that would work with the 486 . . .": "First of all, we positioned it as a coprocessor to the 80486 and made sure that it could be justified on that basis. We designed it as a stand-alone processor, but made it very useful as an accessory to the 486." Comments of Intel designer Les Kohn in "Intel Corporation: Strategy for the 1990s," *Graduate School of Business, Stanford University,* PS-BP-256C, 1991, p. 9.

p. 106. "the advantages of RISC technology over CISC . . .": "For many business applications, CISC may be both faster and cheaper." "The Reality of RISC," *Computer World,* March 22, 1993, p. 72. "It is now clear that those early ads showing RISC on a sharp upward performance curve as CISC leveled off were wishful thinking at best." From an open letter from Michael Slater to the heads of IBM, Motorola and Apple, *OEM Magazine,* July/August 1995, p. 24.

p. 111. Peter F. Drucker: " 'The entrepreneur,' said the French economist J. B. Say around 1800, 'shifts economic resources out of an area of lower and into an area of higher productivity and greater yield.' " Peter F. Drucker, *Innovation and Entrepreneurship: Practice and Principles.* (Bungay, Suffolk: William Heinemann Ltd., 1985), p. 19.

p. 113. Apple's Newton criticized: "Instead of accolades, Newton became a running joke on no less visible a platform than Gary Trudeau's Doonesbury comic strip." "What Apple Learned from the Newton," *Business Week,* November 22, 1993, p. 110.

p. 117. W. Edwards Deming, *Out of the Crisis.* (Cambridge: Massachusetts Institute of Technology Center for Advanced Engineering Study, 1988).

p. 120. Intel's corporate culture: "A business like ours has to employ a management process unlike that used in more conventional industries. If we had people at the top making all the decisions, then these decisions would be made by those unfamiliar with the technology of the day. . . . Since our business depends on what it knows to survive, we mix 'knowledge-power people' with 'position-power people' daily, so that together they make the decisions that will affect us for years to come. We at Intel frequently ask junior members of the organization to participate jointly in a decision-making meeting with senior managers. This only works if everybody at the meeting voices opinions and beliefs as *equals,* forgetting or ignoring status differentials. And it is much easier to achieve this if the organization doesn't separate its senior and junior people with limousines, plush offices and private dining rooms." Andrew S. Grove, quoted in "My Turn: Breaking the Chains of Command," *Newsweek,* October 3, 1983, p. 23.

p. 124. "the sequence of emotions associated with grief . . .": Elisabeth Kubler-Ross, *On Death and Dying* (New York: Macmillan, 1969).

p. 127. "replacement of corporate heads . . .": " 'In many cases, the emotional ties of the career CEO are just too strong,' says Ferdinand Nadherny, vice-chairman of Russell Reynolds Associates, the nation's largest executive recruiting firm. . . . [W]ith the recession creaming Tenneco's 1991 results after years of erratic earnings, the board decided it was time to push aside the proud chief [James L. Ketelsen]. '[Michael H.] Walsh came with a clean perspective,' explains one director. 'He wasn't weighed down by the politics of the past.' " "Tough Times, Tough Bosses," *Business Week,* November 25, 1991, pp. 174–75.

p. 128. "Strategic Dissonance": For further discussion of this phenomenon, see Robert A. Burgelman and Andrew S. Grove, "Strategic Dissonance," *California Management Review,* Vol. 38, No. 2, Winter 1996, pp. 1–20. I also make a parallel to the concept of cognitive dissonance: "New events may happen or new events may become known to a person, creating at least a momentary dissonance with existing knowledge, opinion, or cognition concerning behavior. . . . What, then, are the circumstances that make it difficult for the person to change his actions? 1. The change may be painful or involve loss. . . . 2. The present behavior may be otherwise satisfying. . . . 3. Making the change may simply not be possible." Leon Festinger, *A Theory of Cognitive Dissonance.* (Evanston, IL: Row, Peterson and Company, 1957), pp. 4, 25–27.

p. 133. "Compaq's board of directors . . .": "[A]fter weeks of high-level wrangling aimed at pulling the company out of a six-month decline in revenues, profits, and market share . . . [Compaq Chairman Benjamin M.] Rosen stepped in." "Compaq's New Boss Doesn't Even Have Time to Wince," *Business Week,* November 11, 1991, p. 41.

p. 134. "importance of scale and scope . . .": In his book, *Scale and Scope* (Cambridge, MA: Belknap Press, 1990), Harvard Business School Professor Alfred D. Chandler showed that many industries adapt to a model in which scale and scope end up being key. These historical examples helped us understand what we needed to do.

Chapter 8: Rein in Chaos

p. 141. Lotus in 1985: "By leveraging Lotus' position as a leading supplier of application software, we are continuing to develop a rich line of companion and complementary products." *Lotus 1985 Annual Report*, p. 11.

p. 141. Lotus in 1991: "It's tempting to describe 1991 as a year of transition at Lotus. . . . But our customers' world—and the world of individual users—now opens up onto a broader horizon. In this wider world, users are linked by networks and networked applications, and they share computing resources, information and work itself. [I]n Notes, we have the ground-breaking collaborative computing product that is changing the way companies do business." *Lotus 1991 Annual Report*, pp. 2, 4, 5.

p. 144. "Drucker suggests . . .": Nineteenth-century French economist J. B. Say quoted in Peter Drucker's *Innovation and Entrepreneurship: Practice and Principles:* "An entrepreneur is one who shifts resources from areas of low productivity and yield to areas of higher productivity and yield." *Op. cit.*

pp. 149–50. early movers: see Gary Hamel and C. K. Prahalad, "Competing for the Future," *Harvard Business Review,* July–August 1994, pp. 122–28.

p. 151. "Put all of your eggs . . .": "Behold, the fool saith, 'Put not all thine eggs in the one basket'—which is but a manner of saying, 'Scatter your money and your attention'; but the wise man saith, 'Put all your eggs in one basket and WATCH THAT BASKET.' " Mark Twain, *Puddin'head Wilson,* (New York: Penguin Books, 1986), p. 163. First published in 1894.

p. 158. "Hewlett-Packard decided . . .": "Intel Corp. and Hewlett-Packard Co. shook the core of the computer industry last week when they announced a broad partnership to develop a new generation of microprocessor technology." "Intel-HP Agreement Alters CPU Landscape," *PC Week,* June 13, 1994, p. 1.

p. 159. Dr. Wang's vision: "An Wang was more than just a technical wizard. From the beginning, he thrived on keeping his hands in all aspects of the business, and the management system was perfectly designed to fit his voracious eclectic intellect. 'The Doctor had a whim of iron. He was into everything. He would come into the engineering department, head to the blackboard of a first-level engineer and sketch out what he wanted,' says a former engineer. 'What Dr. Wang wanted then became the design.'" "The Fall of the House of Wang," *Business Month,* February 1990, p. 24.

p. 159. Wang in bankruptcy: "After peaking at $3 billion in revenue in 1988, Wang hit hard times as the PC industry advanced and started to cut into word processors. . . . 'They completely misunderstood the PC industry and it cost them greatly,' [said Stephen Smith, an analyst with Paine Webber, Inc.]." "Wang Files for Chapter 11, Plans to Let Go 5,000," *Computer Reseller News,* August 24, 1992, p. 10

p. 162. "a powerful, adaptive organization . . .": For studies on this subject, see Robert A. Burgelman, "Intraorganizational Ecology of Strategy-making and Organizational Adaptation: Theory and Field Research," *Organization Science,* Vol. 2, No. 3, August 1991. Also *ibid.,* "Fading Memories: A Process Theory of Strategic Business Exit in Dynamic Environments," *Administrative Science Quarterly,* No. 139, 1994.

p. 162. "These debates are vigorous . . .": "The real benefit . . . is to team up people with hands-on knowledge with those in positions of power to create the best solutions in the interest of both." Andrew S. Grove, "My Turn: Breaking the Chains of Command," *Newsweek,* October 3, 1983, p. 23.

p. 162. "supporting the decision . . .": "An organization does not live by its members agreeing with one another at all times on everything. It lives instead by people committing to support the decisions and the moves of the business." Andrew S. Grove, *High Output Management* (New York: Random House, 1983), p. 91.

p. 163. Hewlett-Packard: *Hewlett-Packard 1994 Annual Report,* p. 44.

p. 164. AT&T and regional Bell companies' market valuation: In December 1983, following the breakup, AT&T and the RBOCs had an approximate market valuation of $60 billion. *Capital International Per-*

spective (Capital International S.A., Geneva, Switzerland), January 1984, pp. 330–32. In 1995, their market value was approximately $240 billion. *The Red Herring,* September 1995, pp. 110, 112.

Chapter 9: The Internet: Signal or Noise? Threat or Promise?

p. 167. "the stock skyrocketed . . .": Netscape's initial offering price on August 9, 1995, was $28 a share. It reached a high that day of $74 and subsequently peaked at $174 on December 6, 1995. *Bloomburg Business News.*

p. 167. "creating a dramatized confrontation . . .": " 'There are gales of creative destruction blowing through every corner of the information technology industry, and the source of that wind is the Internet,' says Paul Saffo, a consultant and research fellow at the Institute for the Future in Menlo Park, California." "Whose Internet Is It Anyway?" *Fortune,* December 11, 1995, p. 121.

p. 171. For a more detailed history of the Internet, see Joshua Eddings, *How the Internet Works* (San Francisco: Ziff Davis Press, 1994).

p. 172. "impact the telecommunications industry . . .": "Personal communication over the Internet will overtake telecommunications in five to six years, and telephone operators have the biggest interest in getting into the online business. . . . The importance of the telephone in personal communications will diminish just like the fax has replaced the telex." *Reuters,* February 1, 1996.

p. 174. "impact on the software industry . . .": "From tiny one-person shops to start-ups staffed by prominent Silicon Valley executives, the Net is teeming with new Web software companies. Most wouldn't have a prayer in the conventional software market. But the Net represents a green field where no software maker dominates." "The Software Revolution: The Internet Changes Everything," *Business Week,* December 4, 1995, p. 82. And: "Currently, you have to pay money up front to distribute software through either conventional retail channels or through the large distributors that sell into corporations. On the Internet you don't need these intermediate distribution mechanisms. So we see this potential for low-cost distribution of any kind of intellectual property—whether it be software, or pictures, or movies, or CDs, or anything that can be represented as bits—as one of the most revolution-ary aspects of the Internet." Interview with Jim Clark, *The Red Herring*, November, 1995, p. 70.

p. 174. "won't that siphon off business . . .": "In the computer industry, there's never been a company that's led the way in two succes-sive eras. So really, what Microsoft as a company, or Paul and I as individuals, are trying to do is defy history and actually take our leader-ship from the PC era into this new communications era. The odds are against us, and that's what makes it so much fun and challenging." Bill Gates quoted in "Bill Gates and Paul Allen Talk," Fortune, October 2, 1995, p. 82.

p. 175. "even advertisers are joining in . . .": "Hachette Filipacchi said it has just signed a new media commitment with . . . General Motors." "Hachette Entangles GM in Web for '96," *Wall Street Journal*, November 30, 1995, p. B6.

p. 175. "worldwide spending on advertising . . .": 1995 estimated global spending on advertising was $345.7 billion. *Standard and Poor's Industry Surveys*, October 1995, Vol. 2, New York, p. M15.

p. 178. "Internet appliances": "The device promises to offer the most popular functions of a personal computer, such as sending electronic mail, surfing the Internet and word processing, at a fraction of the cost. There are limitations, however: It's less powerful than a PC, and has no slots to play your own CD-ROMs or software." "Ellison's 'Magic Box,'" *San Francisco Chronicle*, November 16, 1995, p. B1. Also, "The argument is that the day of the desktop application—and therefore the OS—ends when applications are stored and distributed over the Net. . . . Such technology provoked Upside magazine to gush that the Web is a 'whole software standard that makes the current software industry obsolete'" "Dubious Extinction," *PC Week Inside*, November 13, 1995, p. A14.

Index